CULTURES OF AMERICA

JAPANESE AMERICANS

By Lauren Lee

BENCHMARK BOOKS

MARSHALL CAVENDISH

Benchmark Books
Marshall Cavendish Corporation
99 White Plains Road
Tarrytown, New York 10591-9001, U.S.A.

© Marshall Cavendish Corporation, 1996

Edited, designed, and produced by Water Buffalo Books, Milwaukee

For their helpfulness in this project, the author and editors would like to thank Patricia Hyland, Bob Kumaki, Sandra Otaka,
Michael Takada, Lillian Yamada, Sandra Yamate, and Bill Yoshino.

Picture Credits: Sabine Beaupré 1995: 7, 17; © The Bettmann Archive: 32; © Dave Bjorn/Photo Resource Hawaii: 37; ©
John S. Callahan/Photo Resource Hawaii: 43, 47 (top); © Tami Dawson/Photo Resource Hawaii: Cover, 36; © Tim
Holte: 73; © Val Kim/Photo Resource Hawaii: 44, 48; © Richard B. Levine: 75; © Lance Nelson/H. Armstrong Roberts:
8; © Paul M. Perez: 5, 51, 56, 60, 72; © Reuters/Bettmann: 64; © Franco Salmoiraghi/Photo Resource Hawaii: 1, 4, 40,
46, 47 (bottom), 53, 61, 67; © Elliott Smith: 41, 55, 63, 68; © A. Tovy/H. Armstrong Roberts: 6; © UPI/Bettmann: 10,
13, 14, 15, 16, 18, 22, 24, 26, 29, 30, 34, 69, 70 (both), 71 (both), 74; © Jamie Wellner/Photo Resource Hawaii: 54

Library of Congress Cataloging-in-Publication Data

Lee, Lauren, 1963-
    Japanese Americans / by Lauren Lee.
    p.   cm. -- (Cultures of America)
    Includes bibliographical references and index.
    Summary: Provides a history of Japanese immigration to the United States and discusses Japanese customs and
contributions to American culture.
    ISBN 0-7614-0162-8 (lib. bdg.)
    1. Japanese Americans--Juvenile literature. [1. Japanese Americans.] I. Title. II. Series.
    E184.J3L43   1995   95-11025
    973'.04956--dc20   CIP
                                                                                                            AC

To PS – MS
To Julia, Laura, and Anna Takada and to Jeffrey Otaka and Elizabeth Kumaki — LL

Printed in Malaysia
Bound in the U.S.A.

CONTENTS

INTRODUCTION

Japanese Americans are a distinct American group. Among the first Asians to arrive in Hawaii and on the West Coast, they had been accomplished and well educated in their native land. And other than Native and African Americans, they were the only American group to be imprisoned and relocated as a result of a government policy.

After first working in the Hawaiian sugar plantations and California farms, the first Japanese Americans became ready to settle down. They built Buddhist temples, started Japanese restaurants, and staffed schools for their children. They even established graveyards. Although they were denied many rights and privileges because they were nonwhite, they labored diligently to prepare their American-born children for decent lives. When this second generation was young, the entire West Coast population of Japanese Americans was uprooted and sent to prison camps for the duration of World War II, in which the United States fought against Japan. Because the Japanese Americans appeared to be "foreign," U.S. officials feared they would be disloyal. All of them — old people and infants included — were sent to prison. Japanese Americans lost everything: farms, businesses, communities, and, most importantly, their confidence in the American dream.

Following the war, Japanese Americans spread throughout the United States, hoping to blend into the mainstream and avoid being singled out ever again. Many hid their background. As a result, Japanese American culture was weakened. Families lived apart from their relatives, community, and friends, and children learned little Japanese. During the 1970s and 1980s, Japanese Americans began to fight back, demanding and receiving an apology from the government for their wrongful imprisonment.

Most Japanese Americans today are part of the American mainstream. At the same time, small, dedicated groups in many cities work to retain their ethnic heritage. At Japanese Buddhist temples, summer camps, and annual picnics, community members gather. Political and cultural activists struggle to keep their culture alive so that they can pass it on to their children and, ultimately, enrich the culture of the United States.

Oshino Village lies in the shadow of Mt. Fuji. Japan's many mountains, volcanoes, and earthquakes made farming a challenge for Japan's peasant class.

CHAPTER ONE

LEAVING A HOMELAND
LIFE IN OLD JAPAN

In 1901, Hiro Takei looked east at the Pacific Ocean. From his family's farm where he stood, he watched the sunrise. Below the sun, all he could see was water, but he had read of the places beyond what he could see, especially the Hawaiian Islands.

The plantations of Hawaii, which had become a U.S. territory in 1900, were rumored to be filled with gold. Other young men, the oldest in their families, were leaving small, struggling farms, moving to Hawaii to work, and sending money back home to their families. Turning toward his family's home, Hiro thought of the long years of struggle, frustration, and dishonor they had endured. Perhaps it was time for him to leave.

Limited Land and Short Seasons

Hiro was one of thousands of Japanese who left their homeland because of economic and social upheavals during the late nineteenth and early twentieth centuries. To understand the sweeping changes that occurred, it is first necessary to understand the relationship of the Japanese people to the land itself. Japan does not contain much land. It is made up of some three thousand islands, including four large and important ones: Hokkaido, Honshu, Shikoku, and Kyushu. Japan divides the Pacif-

ic Ocean on the east and the Sea of Japan on the west. Japan's north is bordered by Russia's Sakhalin Island and Siberian region. West of the Sea of Japan lie China and the Korean Peninsula.

Today, most Japanese live in the urban areas between the cities of Osaka and Tokyo, but in the past much of Japan's population was made up of farmers who lived in the country on all the islands. During the Meiji Period (from 1868 to 1912, named for the family of reigning Emperor Mutsuhito), when the majority of Japanese moved to the United States, these farmers struggled to keep their land.

Japan is an island nation, with rugged terrain and stark natural beauty. Japanese immigrants came from all the islands, but the first came from rural areas in the southwest.

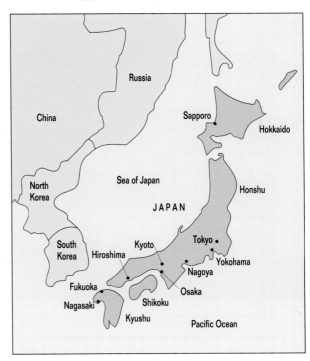

Japan's mountainous geography challenged traditional farmers. One rugged mountain range in central Honshu, called the "Japanese Alps," is made up of volcanic ridges that are sometimes taller than 8,000 feet. Smaller mountain ranges, which reach around 5,500 feet in height, also break up the landscape. There are few flatlands, or plains, for growing crops. Three-quarters of the islands are covered by forests. Volcanoes erupt regularly, and earthquakes are frequent. Rivers are short and flow swiftly.

Cherry blossoms bloom by a pagoda in Kyoto. Japan's short, extreme seasons produce striking landscapes that the people deeply admire.

As a result of Japan's rough geography, Meiji-era farms were small. To survive, farmers have traditionally depended on good weather, constant labor, and fair taxation. Japan's seasons can be extreme: frigid winters, pounding rains, and tropical heat limit the farmers' growing season even today. Although the climate is generally warm, winters can be very cold. Seasonal winds bring heavy snow to the western region, whereas the eastern region has dry, clear winters. When spring comes, it is short, lasting from early March to late May.

That is when Japan's famous plum and cherry blossoms bloom. Farmers must quickly plant their crops before the heavy rainstorms, called typhoons, begin in early spring and summer.

When the typhoons end, a hot and humid summer begins. These conditions are good for growing rice, but farmers must be diligent. Summer in Japan's southwest is tropical for three or four months, like the climate in South Pacific countries like Vietnam or the Philippines. Plants grow to tremendous sizes, and large insects fill the air. Then, in early autumn, the typhoons return. Fall in Japan is beautiful but brief. A cold winter follows.

Before Japan opened its ports to international trade, the farmers' rice crops were especially important to the survival of this densely populated nation. About 120 million people — half the population of the United States — live in a land the size of California. Because taxes rose and farming conditions became more difficult, Japan's farmers had trouble growing enough rice to support its population. This is why, between 1885 and 1924, 200,000 Japanese left for Hawaii, and nearly another 200,000 left for the U.S. mainland.

Isolation

Before the emigration to the United States, Japan was isolated from the rest of the world. It had kept to itself for two and one-half centuries. During the Edo Period, from 1600 to 1867 (named for Edo, the seat of the government), Japan's leaders had shut off the nation to foreign trade and influence by closing its ports. Closing the ports weakened Japan's economy just when the economies of Europe and the United States were gaining strength. But the Edo government resisted all outside influence by outlawing foreign books, religion, and ideas. Christianity, for example, was outlawed by the government because Christian ideas often encouraged Japanese people to challenge traditional values such as obedience and harmony. To stop these influences, the government executed more than three thousand Christians in the 1600s. Over time, the government was successful in keeping out foreign influence. As a result, Japan's own culture developed, although at the cost of lives and freedom.

Meiji-Era Social Classes

Like many other Asian nations, Japan was influenced by the great Chinese philosopher Confucius, who believed that everyone had a position in society. Edo society had four levels: the highest, which was made up of warriors and government workers; the second, made up of peasants; the third, made up of artisans and craftspeople; and the lowest, made up of merchants and other businesspeople. In addition, there were people who did not fit into any category at all but who had very specific status, such as butchers and Buddhist monks. Unlike in the United States, where people liked to find their own place in society, each Japanese person's role was decided at birth based on what his or her parents did for a living.

The Samurai Warriors. The highest class was made up of warriors and civil servants. In the beginning of the Edo Period, when Japanese society was loosely structured, the role of the warriors, or *samurai*, was to defend their masters. But after the government gained control of the nation and the society became stable, the samurai's role became ceremonial. Because there were no wars to fight, they served the royal court or their own masters. The samurai valued complete loyalty to their lord, fierce defense of their status and honor, and fulfillment of all their obligations. Yet the samurai class had its weaknesses.

If, for example, samurai were "masterless," they could be dangerous because their behavior was not easily controlled. With the freedom to make their own decisions, one group of masterless samurai tried to kill Japan's leaders. When they failed, as punishment, all forty-seven masterless samurai were forced to commit suicide with their short daggers. Even samurai with masters could be dangerous. They often used their long, single-edged swords to enforce their power over the majority of the population. If a commoner showed them disrespect, the samurai had the right to kill the commoner on the spot.

Over time, the samurai class became a class of civil servants, or government workers. They became skilled at using the writing brush instead of the sword. Former samurais often studied Confucian philosophy and helped establish schools that many peasants attended.

The Peasants. The peasants were the rice producers of Japan. Even though the word "peasant" suggests that they were all poor, many were landowners, and some even became wealthy. What the peasants had in common

A young man carries newspapers to distribute during the Meiji Period. From 1868 to 1912, reforms to modernize Japan resulted in a high literacy rate, even among the peasants who emigrated to the United States.

But during the 1800s, the rich farm families discovered that they could make more money by spinning cotton, weaving fabric, or brewing sake, a rice-wine drink. Some families abandoned farming to become prosperous merchants. The families who held only small farms were left on their own. Then, when taxes went up, many of the families with small farms had trouble surviving. Their land was the least fertile, and they paid the highest taxes. The rich became richer, and the poor became poorer.

Artisans and Merchants. At the next level were artisans, or craftspeople. Blacksmiths, artists, and potters made finished products that were then sold to other people. During the Edo Period, these artisans lived in the towns, along with merchants. Merchants, or businesspeople, were at the bottom of society during the Edo Period. According to Confucian ideas, making money is not a noble activity, yet it became more and more popular during this era. Eventually, many wealthy merchants influenced Japanese culture by supporting theater, the arts, and the construction of Buddhist temples. By the mid-1800s, being a merchant was gaining status. In fact, many well-off peasant families became merchants.

Other Social Groups. Some people did not fit into the four official rankings. Some ranked above the samurai, others below the merchants. Court aristocrats, Buddhist monks, and Shinto priests had very high status. Losers in warfare and criminals were considered to be

was owning and farming land. Before the Edo Period, they had fairly high status, second only to the samurai class. Families had banded together. Each family contributed labor and in turn received protection and support from the others.

WESTERN INFLUENCE

Beginning around 1868, people from all classes in Japan tried to adapt to Western customs. Japanese townsmen began wearing Western clothes. Instead of bowing, they shook hands. People began taking Western medicines, and the Western calendar was adopted. Mail service was introduced, and Japan began using the metric system. Before the Meiji Period, samurai shaved the top of their heads, allowing the rest of their hair to grow long and tying it into a top knot. This style was replaced by Western-style haircuts. Men began wearing beards and using toothbrushes. Even Buddhist Japan, which traditionally avoided eating meat, invented sukiyaki, a meal consisting of thin slices of beef, bean curd, and vegetables. Many wealthy Japanese added Western-style rooms to their traditional homes. Young people learned Western-style ballroom dancing. But when the government began holding weekly dances in Tokyo for political and diplomatic leaders, conservative Japanese began rejecting Western culture. By the late 1890s, many Western influences had been cast out, and most people reverted to Japanese tradition.

very low. According to Buddhist beliefs, all life is sacred, so those who took life were not allowed to be part of society. Butchers and leatherworkers, who took the lives of animals, were thus outcasts.

The End of Isolation

One major event changed Japanese society, economy, and culture. In 1853, U.S. naval officer Commodore M. C. Perry invaded the Japanese ports and forced them to open up to foreign trade. As a result of this intrusion, the leadership in Japan changed. The Edo emperor was assassinated, and eventually the Meiji emperor took power. It was during the Meiji Period, from 1868 to 1912, that most Japanese emigrants left for Hawaii and North America.

The Meiji leaders decided that Japan had to change quickly in order to make the country richer and the military stronger. Otherwise the West would interfere with their nation. As a result, the government encouraged the growth of business, education, and the military. Factories, ships, and other expensive equipment were needed to allow this growth. Therefore, the government taxed the peasants heavily to pay for these changes.

Sadly, this taxation destroyed many farm families. More than three hundred thousand families lost their lands because they could not make the payments. In order to be honorable, Japanese farmers did everything they possibly could to fulfill their financial obligations. In one village, most of the farmers sold their property to pay their taxes. In one prefecture, or region, the peasants were so poor that in order to survive, they ate the husks of rice and a bean paste liquid mixed with grass.

As a result of these changes, Japan began to have difficulty keeping people from leaving the country, which at the time was against the law. In 1868, the Hawaiian consul general in Japan began to secretly contract laborers. Next, a German merchant took Japanese laborers to a silk farm in California. Finally, in 1884, the Japanese government allowed foreign planters to recruit laborers openly. Recruiters from Hawaiian sugar plantations visited rural areas in southwestern Japan, looking for people willing to leave their homes to work abroad.

THE STORY OF THE PEACH BOY

Once upon a time, there was an old, childless couple who lived on a farm. To be childless was a heavy burden in old Japan, where children were supposed to care for people when they became elderly. One day, the woman went down to the stream to wash clothes. Suddenly, she saw a large peach floating in the water. She brought it home, and her husband cut the fruit open. They were surprised to find a baby boy in the peach. His name was Momotaro. He grew up to be a strong, brave warrior — an expert swordsman, a samurai for the people. He left to fight the monsters who were threatening the village. After destroying the monsters, Momotaro returned home and took care of his parents for the rest of their lives.

The story of the Peach Boy has been told by emigrant parents to their children for decades. Emigrants often did not want to leave their homeland, but they had to in order to fulfill family responsibilities. Even though they lived in the United States, emigrants told the story of the Peach Boy returning to his parents after slaying dragons that threatened their people.

By leaving home and sending money back to their families, the emigrants tried to slay the monster of their parents' poverty, or the dishonor of debt. The story of Momotaro helped the departing Japanese find the courage to go ahead with their journey, holding on to the idea that they would return home some day.

Duties of the Young

Many young people left family farms to find work elsewhere, earn money, and pay off their parents' debts. Obedience to parents, putting family first, and hard work and sacrifice are powerful traditional Japanese values. Sons and daughters were duty bound to fulfill their parents' obligations. When they earned money, whether in a Japanese city, in Hawaii, or in San Francisco, one of the first things they did was send money home.

The oldest male child had an important role in Japanese families. When a land-owning peasant father became too elderly to work, for example, his oldest son would inherit the land. Because of the limited land available in Japan, dividing up small farms among children would make the farms too small to produce enough rice to feed a family. So the boundaries of the farm would stay unchanged, and the oldest son would take charge and become responsible for his parents. The younger sons often left to go to the cities. During the Meiji Period, one politician told first sons to "stay in Japan and be men of Japan. Second sons, go abroad with great ambition as men of the world!"

Working Women

Not only sons helped their parents. Although Japanese society traditionally had kept women in the home to keep house and raise children, their position improved between the 1860s and the 1910s. Emperor Meiji wanted his country to change from old to new ways. He argued that girls should be educated as well as boys. At that time, unlike Chinese and many European women, most Japanese women could read. Japanese girls attended elementary school for six years and middle school for two years. Many then attended high school for four years, studying English, Japanese, mathematics, literature, writing, and religion. With the Meiji educational reforms, all Japanese children

ONE JAPANESE PEASANT FAMILY

The economic and cultural changes affected most Japanese families, such as that of young Shiba Takada. One day in 1884, Shiba woke up with a heavy heart. He folded up his futon, or thin mattress, and walked barefoot to the main room. There he sat near the heater and talked with his parents about their family's debt. His mother served him watery rice in a bowl, and he ate it hungrily. When he handed the bowl back to her, he smiled, so that she would think he was full. Before the taxes went up, the family had eaten rice, fish, vegetables, soup, and pickles. Shiba's stomach growled with the memory of earlier meals. After putting the bowl away, his mother straightened her simple kimono robe, made of coarse cotton and tied in the front, and sat on her heels next to her husband and son.

Shiba knew that, unlike the young people in many peasant families, he had many choices. After all, he could read, and his family had owned their farm for centuries. They were not used to being poor. But now, his father could not pay their bills. As the only son, Shiba was duty bound to protect his parents' honor. He would leave for the city to work and send money home. He bowed to his parents, put on his coat, walked across the straw mats, and slid open the rice-paper door. Outside, he put on his shoes, looked at his tile-roofed house for the last time, and began walking to the city. He would work in a factory to pay off his parents' debts.

Girls spin thread for weaving fabric. Many women left traditional spinning at home in order to labor in Japan's new, modern factories.

In the 1950s, Japanese girls are learning to perform the tea ceremony while a boy watches. In earlier periods, the ceremony was performed only by men, but Japanese culture has changed over a long time.

learned about foreign countries in an effort to help the nation move forward.

Because of the family and cultural tradition that favored boys, many girls felt ready to leave the family farms. An old Japanese saying encouraged parents to have three children: "One to sell, one to follow, and one in reserve." The one to follow was the eldest son, who would inherit the family's farm. He and his wife, along with any unmarried children in the family, would live with his parents. The one in reserve was the second son, whose role was to support the parents if the first son was unable. The one to sell was the daughter. When she married, she became a member of her husband's family. The Japanese used to say that the "womb was borrowed," meaning that the purpose of a woman's body was to provide sons for her husband's family. If a bride failed to provide children, she might be returned to her parents. In a wealthy family, the husband might wed a second wife to produce children if the first wife could not.

Western ideas, including women's rights, Christianity, and democracy, began changing women's role in Japan. Young Japanese women decided to help their own parents and use their education to travel in foreign lands. Many of the young women had studied English and were thus interested in going to the United States. Soon women were leaving home to work almost as often as men. Most of them stayed in Japan but moved to the cities, where they worked in factories. In the 1880s, for example, daughters of farming families provided four-fifths of the labor in the textile industry. They worked as weavers, spinners, and dyers of cloth.

Women also worked in tea- and paper-processing factories. They carried heavy loads at construction sites and in coal mines. They served food and beer in inns. By 1900, 60 percent of Japan's industrial workers were women. When stories describing Hawaii as "heavenly" came back to Japan, these English-speaking, hard-working women became interested. Many agreed to go to Hawaii through marriages arranged by their families, which was a common custom in Japan at the time. The men in Hawaii wanted them to come as well. Two incomes could pay off family debts faster than one, they felt. Plus, women improved their quality of life, and at that time Japanese men could not marry Caucasian women without being banned from their families.

Leaving Japan

By the late 1800s, Japan was a different place than it had been under isolation. The farmers were almost literally losing the ground they stood on. Western influences introduced foreign ideas to Japan. Travel became legal, emigration became possible for the first time, and Americans visited Japan in increasing numbers. Due to foreign influences, educational reforms, and increased commerce, the Japanese social structure slowly began to change. Peasants, including women, were more educated than ever before. They had a sense of the possibilities that were open to them as individuals, not just as members of a family with fixed roles and responsibilities. Making money as a merchant did not carry the same shame that it once did. When the farmers' difficulties continued, and the recruiters began weaving tales about a heavenly life filled with riches in Hawaii, many peasants were ready to listen.

Mt. Fuji towers over a Japanese farming community early in the century. Many of the young Japanese peasants who left their homes and established family farms in the United States found it difficult to leave behind the towns where their ancestors had lived for centuries.

This elderly Japanese American man, photographed in 1942, sailed to Hawaii as a young man with the first group of immigrants in 1885.

CHAPTER TWO

LIFE IN A NEW LAND
DIFFICULT SETTLEMENT IN THE NEW WORLD

Young Japanese emigrant men hoped for a successful future in the United States. At the same time, though, they felt sadness at leaving their homeland and sensed the risk involved in their trip. To express their feelings they wrote a traditional type of poetry called *haiku*. The following unrhymed, three-line verses reveal their hopefulness and fear:

> Huge dreams of fortune
> Go with me to foreign lands,
> Across the ocean.

> Family fortunes
> Fall into the wicker trunk
> I carry abroad.

Although many emigrants eventually became successful, the trip to the United States turned out to be much more difficult than they could have imagined.

Who Were the Immigrants?

Most Japanese emigrants began moving to the United States around 1880. Although

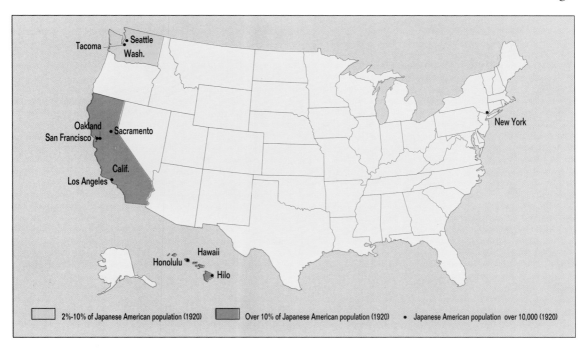

2%-10% of Japanese American population (1920) Over 10% of Japanese American population (1920) • Japanese American population over 10,000 (1920)

Most Japanese immigrated to Hawaii, California, Washington, and Oregon. Although some immigrants slowly moved inland, most did not leave the West Coast until the World War II internment of Japanese Americans in prison camps ended in 1945.

Young Japanese immigrants arrive in San Francisco by ocean liner in 1920. By 1920, male Japanese immigrants had established farms, businesses, and communities. Many sent for their wives and children as they began to settle into American life.

some emigration continues today, most Japanese Americans are descended from those who came before 1924. Between 1885 and 1924, 200,000 Japanese settled in Hawaii and 180,000 on the U.S. mainland. Hawaii, which became a U.S. territory in 1900, was the emigrants' first stop because recruiters from Hawaiian sugar plantations had invited many Japanese to the islands. Although some Japanese later moved to the mainland United States, emigration stopped in 1908 as a result of a U.S. federal law that kept Japanese from moving to the mainland from Hawaii. Consequently, Hawaii today has a high percentage of Japanese Americans in its population, unlike the mainland. Similarly, the history of Japanese immigrant life differs between the mainland and the islands.

Because the Japanese government wanted only positive examples of Japanese to represent their country abroad, it decided who could leave. The first emigrants to the United States were young men, primarily in their twenties and thirties. The Japanese government required that these emigrants be healthy and literate and have about eight years of schooling. So most of them were better educated than many other Japanese people. In fact, the emigrants' literacy rate was higher than that of European immigrants to the United States. Most were from farms in southwestern Japan, and although their families struggled financially, most emigrants were not desperately poor. The Japanese government hoped that such high-quality emigrants could ensure respect for their nation in the United States.

Why They Left

As we learned in Chapter One, most emigrants went to Hawaii to earn money to pay off their family debts. By spending as little money as possible, most planned to save approximately one thousand dollars in three years. When they returned to Japan, this money would allow their parents to buy back lost land and get out of debt.

Unfortunately, high living expenses and other problems kept many Japanese emigrants from reaching their goals as quickly as they had planned. Many who came to Hawaii and the U.S. mainland to work, intending to return to Japan someday, ended up staying.

Others planned to stay longer to earn money to buy more land in Japan for themselves, but only after they first took care of their parents' needs. Although social status in Japan was usually fixed by birth, there were ways to improve one's status. One way for a young man to accomplish that was to be adopted by his wife's family. Sometimes, wealthy or samurai-class families had daughters but no sons. By adopting their daughter's husband (instead of following the tradition of the wife joining her husband's family), the wife's family could make sure that their name would survive. Adopted husbands, known as *yoshis*, took on the name of the wife's family and passed that family's name and higher status on to their children. A young man, however, had to offer something in return for his improved status. Usually, he was from a successful farming family with large land holdings that became part of his wife's family's property.

Some young Japanese men went to the United States to try earning enough money to buy large farms so they could be adopted by a higher-status family on their return. This tradition was followed more often by second sons, who did not carry the responsibility of passing on their own family name.

Other young Japanese men left home because they wanted to avoid going off to war.

In 1905, for example, war broke out between Russia and Japan. Because the war was unpopular, many Japanese families hid their eighteen-year-old sons so they would not have to fight. One emigrant quickly applied for his passport and left Japan two weeks after his eighteenth birthday. Unlike the sons of farming families, he had no plan for his future in the United States. He was simply happy to escape going to war. When he arrived in the United States, he took any job he could find and, like many immigrants, never returned to Japan.

Other emigrants wanted to be free of the strict rules that controlled the lives of all Japanese. Second sons and women had lower status in Japanese culture and felt restricted in their opportunities at home. Duties to family and limitations on women frustrated some Japanese. Like other immigrants to the United States, many Japanese, particularly those with lower status and fewer opportunities, wanted a chance to be free of traditional constraints and to prove themselves.

Recruiting by Hawaiian Plantation Owners

Hawaiian sugar plantation owners turned to Japan for labor because Japanese peasants knew farming, were disciplined, and needed income. One of the most active of these recruiters was the owner of a large Japanese trading company operating in Hawaii; during the 1870s, he began recruiting workers from southwestern Japan. As recruiters spread the word about Hawaii's lovely climate and high salaries, one emigrant remarked that life in Hawaii sounded like heaven. Others saw the high salaries as a solution to their families' troubles. Rumors spread quickly throughout this region of Japan, and soon a fever to emigrate spread as well.

Between 1885 and 1894, Japanese emigrants signed contracts to work in Hawaii. According to the contracts, the planters agreed to pay for their passage by ship to Hawaii, and the laborers agreed to work for three years for nine dollars a month plus food, lodging, and medical care. This wage was about six times more than a day laborer could earn in Japan. The workers would be able to save about four hundred yen, nearly enough for some of them to marry into a higher-status family. For others, it would be enough money to help their parents buy more land.

In 1885, six hundred emigrants out of twenty-eight thousand applicants took the first ship from Japan to Hawaii. More laborers applied to emigrate. By 1894, thirty thousand Japanese had come to the Hawaiian Islands as contract laborers.

After 1894, emigrants came to the Hawaiian Islands as private laborers, paying for their own passage or borrowing money for the trip. Some families took out loans against the value of their farms or borrowed from moneylenders to send a son to the United States. They believed it was a good investment.

The Crossing

The Japanese emigrants came to Hawaii on steamships, a rough passage that lasted between ten and twelve days. Terrible smells from vomit, paint (if the ships were new), and unclean bathrooms filled the passenger quarters. Such awful odors ruined the passengers' appetites. Many lost weight. In the beginning, there were few women because most of the male emigrants were financially unable to support families. Many planned to return home in three years to start their families in Japan. Later, the emigrants slept in beds on racks, with separate sections for women and men.

Upon their arrival in Hawaii, some new-comers paid an entrance tax of three dollars that was later ruled illegal plus a two-dollar fee for being in Hawaii. New arrivals were sent to quarantine stations, where they were isolated from the Hawaiian population for a few days or even longer until they passed a physical examination. Most immigrants were sent straight to the plantations.

Hawaiian Plantation Life

Even though Chinese laborers were already in Hawaii and Korean and Filipino laborers were yet to come, the Japanese recruitment was the most successful: By the 1920s, 42 percent of Hawaii's population was of Japanese descent.

Life on the plantations was difficult. A screaming siren awakened laborers at five o'clock in the morning. Workdays lasted ten long hours. The laborers cut cane, hoed weeds, and stripped leaves from sugarcane stalks. Some laborers worked in the steaming-hot sugar mills, where large, loud machines crushed the sugar cane and boiled its juices into molasses and sugar. Workers were hot, tired, and badly treated.

Asian laborers, most of them Japanese, worked under white bosses, usually Portuguese or Spanish. The bosses, or *lunas*, believed that because they were white, they were members of a stronger race whose duty was to supervise weaker Asian laborers. Laws kept nonwhites from taking leadership positions. As a result, most Japanese workers were field hands and mill laborers.

In addition to the sting of discrimination, the laborers felt other, more physical pain. One worker said that if they talked too much, the luna cracked his whip near their heads. Moreover, the laborers were fined for various mistakes: Breaking a wagon by accident cost the laborer five dollars; being disrespectful to the

ORGANIZING WORKERS IN HAWAII

During the Japanese Americans' earliest days in Hawaii, they contributed to the well being of other laboring groups by organizing unions to fight for the fair treatment of workers. Despite efforts by plantation owners to divide up ethnic groups, some Japanese-led unions learned to strike in order to demand better wages and conditions.

In 1919, after a series of strikes by Japanese Americans, a combined group of Japanese and Filipino ethnic laborers demanded higher wages, an eight-hour day, an insurance fund, and paid maternity leave.

Despite using many creative tactics, the strikers lost their bid for improved conditions. But the laborers all learned an important lesson: In addition to the Filipinos and Japanese, Spanish, Portuguese, and Chinese workers had joined in during the strike. All of these ethnic groups had learned the value of working together; they renamed their union the Hawaii Laborers' Association. The Japanese laborers helped lead the way to working-class dignity, inter-ethnic cooperation, and an American identity that went beyond race.

luna could cost one dollar; being caught gambling resulted in a five-dollar fine. For men earning a dollar a day, these fines were devastating. Laborers who refused to work could be fined, arrested, or have their wages docked. Others were kicked, slapped, or whipped. One manager said that disobedient "Japs" should be whipped, for these people have "no feelings except through the hide," like draft animals who were used to pull heavy loads.

The workers wore brass disks around their necks that were stamped with their identification numbers. When the lunas called the laborers, they would call out "7209!" or "1106!" instead of using the person's name. Such treatment was humiliating for men who came from villages where their families had been established for centuries. Not surprisingly, many laborers compared plantation life to prison life.

Planters kept wages low by paying different rates to different ethnic groups. In one camp, the Japanese were paid only $18.00 a month compared to $22.50 a month for Portuguese laborers. Struggling to save money, many Japanese laborers grew their own veg-

etables or fished on local beaches in order to have more food. The managers believed that dividing ethnic groups would allow them to keep all the wages low. Their plan backfired. As a result of these conditions, Japanese laborers fought back and organized unions among the different ethnic groups to demand better conditions and pay.

In the meantime, Japanese culture flourished on the islands. Some workers brought over their families and settled into communities. United by their experiences, these families prepared Japanese food, built Buddhist temples, and even organized baseball leagues. During traditional Japanese holidays, they celebrated as a group and refused to work. In time, many men who brought wives started having children. Workers, both women and men, sacrificed to send their children to school. The first group of Japanese laborers put down roots in Hawaii that remain strong today. Americans of Japanese descent used to be in the majority in Hawaii, but with migration of Caucasians from the mainland and intermarriage with other ethnic groups, the Japanese

American population is now less than 50 percent.

Not all the Japanese felt satisfied on the Hawaiian islands. Some gambled and drank to forget their frustrations. About 55 percent, or more than one hundred thousand people, returned to Japan, although most spent longer in Hawaii than they had planned. Others deserted the plantations for life elsewhere in the United States. Some went to Honolulu, and others went to the mainland.

Picture Brides and Other Women

In time, many Japanese women began to emigrate as well to join the men who had come earlier as laborers. By 1905, Japanese women made up 22 percent of the Japanese American population in Hawaii and 7 percent on the mainland. In 1908, an informal, or "gentlemen's," agreement between the United States

and Japan limited the emigration of Japanese laborers, but the parents, wives, and children of laborers already in the United States were allowed to come. Between 1908 and 1924, nearly sixty-seven thousand Japanese women came to Hawaii. As the population of Japanese women immigrants grew, by 1911 women made up nearly 40 percent of all Japanese immigrants.

About one-quarter of the female immigrants were picture brides, in the Japanese tradition of arranged marriages. Because the Japanese culture is based on family concerns rather than individual choice, marriages were arranged for the good of the family. *Baishakunin*, or matchmakers, helped to select marriage partners. In the Japanese custom of arranged marriages, go-betweens used pictures to show the potential spouse what their counterpart looked like before the first meeting took

Japanese picture brides smile from the deck of the ocean liner *Rakuyo Maru*. Many Japanese women came to the United States in search of a better life through these arranged marriages.

place. This same practice continued in the United States, but the women hoped for more freedom in the States.

Many of the picture brides had held laborer jobs and were able to read. The women had traveled in Japan, lived independently, and knew about the larger world. They were ready to go to North America, so they agreed to marry the men in the pictures. But the pictures did not always tell the truth. The men often sent pictures of themselves at a much younger age, and sometimes they lied about their jobs. When some of the picture brides arrived at the ports in the United States, they could not recognize their husbands from the pictures. Although the men claimed to be businessmen, some were in fact laborers who carried sleeping rolls on their backs. Some women became so depressed that they committed suicide. Others were unfaithful to their husbands. Although many of the picture brides suffered, few were able to return to Japan. Some could not afford the return passage. Others could not bear to face the loss of dignity they would suffer if they fled their husbands and tried to return to their parents' homes.

Most of the picture brides decided to stay in the United States. They made the immigrant community stable and improved its morale. Many of them became working mothers who earned salaries in addition to raising their children and running their homes. Hawaiian officials could not help but notice that Japanese men worked better and seemed happier when their wives were with them. Their presence was so beneficial that the Hawaiian government actively sought Japanese women to emigrate. The women felt their situation was better because they were able to avoid living with their mothers-in-law and were in charge of their own homes, unlike the typical arrangement in Japan.

Women did not emigrate only as picture brides. Thousands of Japanese women also sailed to Hawaii between 1894 and 1908 as contract laborers. They were cooks, seamstresses, and field laborers. They received six dollars per month in wages, compared to ten dollars per month for the men.

Not all the Japanese women were married. Hundreds or thousands — the numbers are not clear — were brought over as prostitutes. Some were sold by poor families; others were kidnapped or tricked into leaving their homes. Recruiters promised young girls that they could pick up gold nuggets on riverbanks in the United States. One woman went aboard a ship in Japan just to see what it was like; when she was ready to go home, the ship had already begun sailing out of port. A sailor brought meals to her room on the ship. When the ship arrived in San Francisco, the sailor dragged her to a house where she was forced to become a prostitute. Pool houses and prostitution rings were part of life in some Japanese neighborhoods, often called Japantowns.

After 1900, with Hawaii now a U.S. territory, Japanese women began arriving on the mainland in greater numbers. By 1909, after the Gentlemen's Agreement limited male immigration, Japanese women immigrants outnumbered men immigrants. By the time a "Ladies' Agreement" halted the emigration of picture brides and other women from Japan in 1921, some twenty thousand Japanese women had come to the United States.

An Early End to Immigration

Unlike immigration from Europe, which continued through the early decades of the twentieth century through the present, Japanese immigration came to a halt early in the century. Many factors contributed to slowing and halting Japanese immigration to the United

Some Asian American children are sitting happily with other Americans in a San Francisco classroom shortly after the end of World War II. In the early 1900s, Asian Americans in San Francisco were forced to attend segregated schools, and for much of World War II, many of their families were the targets of hostility by Anglo neighbors and were confined to prison camps by the U.S. government.

States, but racial discrimination was the leading reason.

On April 18, 1906, San Francisco experienced an earthquake and fire that damaged many school buildings. Because of the shortage of buildings, officials were forced to move Asian American children out of their regular, segregated schools into those ordinarily attended exclusively by white children. The parents of these white children were not happy about their children attending school with Asian children.

The San Francisco School Board included members of the Asiatic Exclusion League, a group devoted to keeping Asians out of American life. Board members argued that children of the "Mongolian race" were evil, vicious, and

immoral, and they ordered Japanese American children to attend Chinatown's segregated schools, even though more than one-quarter of the children were born in the United States. The powerful Japanese government protested the segregation. President Theodore Roosevelt, under pressure from the international political community, persuaded the school board to revoke its segregation order. In return, President Roosevelt signed an order in 1907 prohibiting Japanese laborers in Hawaii, Canada, and Mexico from entering the United States. As a result, Hawaii — which had not yet become a U.S. state — was no longer a source for Japanese immigration, and the number of Japanese coming to the U.S. mainland dropped dramatically.

Finally, all Japanese immigration, including that of picture brides, was halted. In 1924, the Immigration Act, also known as the Oriental Exclusion Act, became law. By that time, around 400,000 Japanese had entered Hawaii or the U.S. mainland, but many had returned to Japan. Nearly 250,000 Japanese Americans remained in U.S. territory. More than half resided in Hawaii, and the 110,000 who lived on the mainland lived in California, where they struggled to build lives and communities but encountered many difficulties.

Life on the Mainland

When Japanese immigrants first moved to the mainland from Hawaii, they passed through Angel Island, an immigration station. Here they spent several days being processed for settlement in the United States. At Angel Island, where the thick walls were covered with three layers of wire netting and meals often consisted of foul-smelling rice, many immigrants felt as if they had been put into a prison.

Once these new arrivals were allowed out of Angel Island and moved to the mainland, most of them settled on the West Coast. This first generation of Japanese immigrants to the mainland were the *Issei*.

The Issei in California and the West Coast

San Francisco Area. By 1904, about ten thousand Japanese, about one-quarter of the mainland Japanese American population, lived in San Francisco. Because farming was a common occupation around San Francisco at the time, many Japanese immigrants became farm workers. As their numbers increased, Japanese Americans formed a business district that in 1908 included supply stores, pool halls, a steam laundry, restaurants, a barbershop, lodging houses, sweet shops and ice cream parlors,

SURPRISING REACTIONS TO THE IMMIGRANTS

An Issei who was used to struggling in Hawaii was nevertheless shocked at his treatment by whites in California: "It was March or April of 1905 when I landed in San Francisco. A man from a Japanese inn was at the port to meet me with a one-horse carriage. There was a gang of scoundrels who came to treat the immigrants roughly as soon as they heard some Japanese had docked. There were a group of fifteen to twenty youngsters who shouted, 'Let's go! The Japs have come!' We rushed to the inn to avoid being hit. As we went along, we were bombarded with abuses such as 'Japs.' They even picked horse dung off the street and threw it at us. I was baptized with horse dung. This was my very first impression of America."

An educated Issei farmer described his experiences with name-calling: "We were living in the countryside; therefore, we experienced less hostility than those in the cities. Once you were out in the cities, it was all different. Being called 'Japs' was almost an everyday occurrence for us. Hardly anybody — maybe with the exception of women — called us 'Japanese' as clearly as it should be said. Some people commented, 'Please don't be offended if we say "Jap." It's only a word. It's almost an abbreviation by stopping at "p" when we are supposed to say "Japanese." So just take it as such and don't be offended.' But, of course, it is still distasteful to us anyway. So I used to tell them, 'We don't hear it that way at all.'"

— From Ronald Takaki's history of Asian Americans, *Strangers from a Different Shore*.

A Japanese American boy sits proudly on a tractor on his family's San Francisco farm in the early 1900s. Before Japanese Americans were allowed to own their own farms, many immigrant farmers bought land in the names of their American-born children.

trade companies, and a bank. Frequently, husbands and wives worked together to run the family business. In addition, the wives were also responsible for all the housework.

Nearby in Chinatown were fourteen gambling houses and a number of prostitution houses, which were visited by many young, unmarried Japanese men. But most Issei men and women created other opportunities for recreation.

The professions of the Issei were varied. Within the community, Japanese immigrants worked as operators of small businesses. Many worked as newspaper publishers and employees, dealers of small trinkets, and owners of Japanese or Western restaurants. Those who worked outside the community became employees of white-owned stores or worked as factory laborers, sailors, cleaners, and houseboys.

The highest number (about one-third) were domestic workers. About fifteen hundred worked in hotels and boarding houses, contributing to a stereotype of Asian Americans working as houseboys for white families.

Most Issei laborers, however, did not enjoy working for someone else. By 1900, some immigrants leased farmland and paid their rent with a percentage of the harvest. As a result of this system and good farming, by 1910, California Issei owned, leased, contracted, or shared nearly two hundred thousand acres.

Spreading Throughout California. Diligent Issei workers fanned out across the California farmland and coast. In the 1890s, they worked around Sacramento, Fresno, and the Pajaro Valley. After the turn of the century, Issei migrated to Southern California to work as railroad and farm laborers. Eventually, Los Angeles' Japantown became the center of the largest concentration of Japanese Americans in the United States. By 1910, in Orange and Imperial counties, the Japanese Americans had made their presence known. Some Japanese Americans began work as commercial fishers around Sacramento, the San Joaquin Valley, and the Monterey Bay area. In Southern California, they harvested abalone; in the north, they fished for salmon. Their fishing methods influenced the tuna fishing industry.

Others became dairy farmers. Unfortunately, these farmers struggled particularly hard. Because they were Asian, the immigrants were not eligible for U.S. citizenship. But unless they were citizens, they could not own land even though they outlabored their American competitors by living more cheaply, working longer hours, and saving more money. As they became more interested in settling in the United States permanently, the Japanese immigrants began buying land in the name of their American-born children, who were automatic citizens by birth.

Overall, the Issei who lived in California were hard working, adaptable, and often successful immigrants. Part of the reason for the Issei farmers' success was their wives' diligence and sacrifice. Often, after sending for picture brides, the farmers built humble homes and began having children. The new families lived in crude "huts" with oil lamps, boards nailed together for tables, and straw-filled beds. Often, wind blew in through cracks in the walls. Life was hard for both husband and wife, but especially for the wife. Wives worked stooped over in the fields from dawn until dusk. One woman arose at 4:30 A.M. to prepare breakfast and worked so hard every day that her weight dropped from 150 to 85 pounds.

A woman's day typically included awakening the children, preparing breakfast, watering plants, sorting vegetables, and, finally, going to sleep between midnight and 1:30 in the morning. Women performed all this work in addition to laboring in the fields with their husbands. The men, known as "Meiji men" after the leadership in power in Japan at the time they had left, would not so much as glance at housework or child care. They would not change a diaper, split firewood, or let their wives sleep before they did. It was a Japanese custom for women to do all work inside the home.

The Pacific Northwest and Alaska. The third major area where Japanese Americans settled was the Pacific Northwest. Some began in Seattle and Tacoma as gang laborers while others worked in Seattle-area sawmills. Some Issei began their families there. In Oregon, where the Japanese population was smaller than in either California or Washington, Issei worked on railroads and in lumber mills, salmon canneries, and farms. Oregon was accustomed to the contributions of Chinese laborers, so it was a less discriminatory environment for the Japanese immigrants.

Other, younger Issei worked seasonal jobs in salmon canneries that extended as far north as Alaska. When the summer canning season was over, many Northwest workers drifted south to California. These drifting laborers were known as "Alaska Boys." Eventually, younger, second-generation Japanese Americans — the *Nisei* — took over these canning jobs as summer work to earn money for college. Later, around World War II, those jobs were taken over by Filipino and Mexican workers.

By 1920, approximately 90,000 of the 110,000 Japanese on the U.S. mainland lived on the West Coast. About one-quarter were citizens by birth. The population was becoming more stable. Some scholars call the period after 1920 the "settling period," and a slogan began making its way around Japanese American communities: "Stay in America and make it your country." So even former sojourners sent for their families and looked for other ways to make the United States their home. They looked for permanent work and laid down their roots. They began to learn English, adapt to U.S. customs, and fit into American life.

Inland and East Coast Life

For many Japanese railroad laborers, their work took them inland to different states in the mainland United States. The work was dangerous and hard. Grave markers for Japanese laborers lie along railroad lines in Montana, Wyoming, Colorado, and Utah. From the Pacific Northwest, many worked the rail lines as gang laborers into Idaho, Montana, and the Dakotas. From there, the Issei traveled south and east. In the meantime, some earlier immigrants who began as students on the East Coast had settled in the nation's biggest cities.

Once they arrived in the interior states, Japanese immigrants took up different kinds of work. Most were laborers or ran small businesses in the Japanese American communities. In Utah, for example, Japanese Americans worked as sugar beet cultivators or operated small businesses. Life in Utah was pleasant but limiting. The Mormons, Utah's dominant religious group, did not discriminate against the Japanese overtly, but opportunities for non-Mormons were limited. In Colorado, some Japanese Americans were self-employed farmers, and others built roads, highways, and dams. A Japanese American community sprang up near Denver's Chinatown, with Buddhist temples, Japanese-style Christian churches, and Japanese-language newspapers. Japanese Amer-

icans worked as sugar beet farmers in Idaho, as meat packers in Nebraska, and as coal miners in Wyoming.

Further east, some laborers moved to Wisconsin to work as ice cutters or railroad hands. In the upper Midwest, where Asians were fewer in number and less of a threat to other workers, they were treated with less prejudice than on the West Coast. In a Wisconsin government report, Issei laborers were described as having "better character than the Belgians and Russians. As laborers they are efficient, energetic, sober, and flexible. They are cleanly in personal habits, wear good-quality clothes, and eat high-quality food. They are thrifty and ambitious. Japanese are regarded at one factory as one of the most desirable class of immigrants ever admitted to the United States."

In the South, well-off Issei established businesses in Texas and farms in Florida. Their challenges in Texas were not usually based on race. Discrimination in Texas usually focused on Latinos and African Americans, so Japanese Americans found themselves classified as whites. They helped develop the rice-farming industry in Texas. Others established fruit orchards, truck farms (where produce was brought to market by truck), or cotton farms. But the land did not support their rice farming, so many left Texas. They farmed in Florida as well, but with mixed success because of competition with Cuban growers. Other Florida Japanese American farmers found success, as they had in California, growing and selling vegetables to markets in other states.

The Japanese had been attending schools on the East Coast for years before the need for laborers began bringing other Japanese to the West from Hawaii. Most scholars were serious young men with a sense of mission who created a good impression of their culture. At first, most returned to Japan. Those who came later always intended to stay, unlike many Japanese immigrants on the West Coast. These East Coast immigrants often worked in lowly positions, such as servants, until they could begin professional careers. Some established firms that traded between Japan and the United States. They imported silk goods, Japanese handicrafts, and tea. Their professions ranged from trade to academics, from restauranting to housecleaning. The East Coast Japanese population remained small, however: only after 1900 did their numbers exceed one thousand.

This sign bars Asian immigrants from farm work. For much of the twentieth century, laws prohibited Japanese immigrants from becoming citizens or purchasing their own land.

Pushed Outside of the Mainstream

At first, many Issei tried to work in the mainstream U.S. economy. They were not welcomed, however. In 1890, a group of Japanese shoemakers lost their jobs because of pressure by the Boot and Shoemakers' White Labor League. In 1906, the U.S. Attorney General ordered the federal courts to deny citizenship to Japanese immigrants. In 1913, the California legislature passed a law outlawing land ownership by Japanese immigrants. One immigrant took his argument for citizenship to the U.S. Supreme Court. His request was denied because he was "not Caucasian." By 1924, immigration by Asians was outlawed completely.

Because Japanese Americans were a racial as well as an ethnic minority, they received unwanted attention from their mainstream neighbors. There were few Asians in general, and in California, for example, the Japanese made up only 2 percent of the population. Although Japanese Americans were able to work as farm and railroad laborers, they were not welcomed into mainstream society. Curses, such as "Jap Go Home," "Yellow Jap!" and "Dirty Jap!" hurt the new immigrants. Some Japanese Americans were spat upon; others were told that they could not buy houses in certain neighborhoods.

As a result of this discrimination, the Japanese were forced to form separate communities to survive in a hostile environment. The Issei developed a separate economy and culture outside the mainstream. They sent their children to Japanese schools, visited Japanese-owned businesses, and belonged to Japanese community organizations. They lived near one another and socialized together. They did not marry non-Japanese, shop at their stores, or attend their schools. Because some Issei planned to return to Japan and others felt unwelcome in the United States, many kept

This Issei, or first-generation, immigrant couple serves a traditional Japanese lunch to a man in Chicago's Japantown. Prior to World War II, most Japanese Americans lived on the West Coast. After the war, many moved inland.

the white community viewed them as "outsiders" who could never become Americans. Thus, they were pushed even further away from mainstream society.

Settling in

Income from their successful small businesses and farms allowed Japanese Americans to support themselves and their own community. In 1925, nearly half the employed Japanese were farmers or farm workers. They sold their produce in Los Angeles, Sacramento, Fresno, and San Francisco. About 70 percent of the produce stalls in Los Angeles in 1909 were Japanese owned. The income that came to the Japanese from the mainstream communities supported Japanese-owned businesses and helped build a solid Japanese American society.

The Issei created social groups based on different interests. Regional clubs started up. Religious organizations ranged from Gospel to Buddhist to Anglican. English schools were set up for immigrants, and Japanese schools were set up for their children. Professional associations brought together tailors, shoe repairers, servants, barbers, and restaurant owners. Clubs for students and at least one residence for women allowed other groups to get together. The immigrants celebrated Japanese holidays throughout the year. At the same time, many Japanese immigrants began to adapt to U.S. culture as well. Instead of thinking of themselves as sojourners, or visitors, they began to settle here. Issei farmers grew crops, sent for wives, and raised children.

up their relationship to Japan. Many second-generation Japanese Americans held dual citizenship, American and Japanese. Some Issei sent their children to Japan to be educated. These individuals were called *Kibei,* meaning American-born but Japanese-educated.

The result of this banding together was the development of "Japantowns" throughout the West Coast. Unfortunately, the more the Issei formed Japanese-like environments, the more

The Second Generation: Becoming an American

The children of the Issei — the Nisei — experienced the same problems as their parents had. In 1927, the Nisei made up about 27 percent of the mainland Japanese American community. Ten years later, half of all Japanese Americans were American born. By 1940, right before World War II began, 63 percent of Japanese Americans were American citizens by birth. Because after 1908 Japanese men were not allowed to immigrate to the mainland from Japan, the Issei, or first generation, stopped growing and an age gap developed between generations. In 1930, the average Nisei was ten years old, and the average Issei was around forty. Most Nisei grew up with parents who were farmers or shopkeepers, and their parents did not want their children to experience the same limitations they had. So the Issei sent their children to the best schools they could, sacrificing their own needs and goals in the interests of their children.

The Nisei lived in two different worlds. They heard the story of the Japanese Peach Boy (see page 12) but also knew Jack and the Beanstalk. They attended Japanese summer dances and weekend jitterbug dances; they celebrated Christmas and New Year's Day as well as the birthday of the Japanese Emperor. They recited the Pledge of Allegiance. Perhaps most important, they Americanized their names: Makoto became Mac; Isamu became Sam. At school, they learned about George Washington, but at home they learned about honor, loyalty, service, and obligation. They attended U.S. public schools, where they jumped and yelled, and Japanese language school, where they were modest and timid. Despite being ethnically pure Japanese, many Nisei felt that they were half American. As a result, they wanted the same things other Americans wanted.

Yet despite going to the best colleges, the Nisei were denied the opportunity to work in the mainstream. In Los Angeles in 1940, because of discrimination in the business world, only 5 percent were employed in white-owned businesses. Only 25 percent of the 160 Nisei who graduated from the University of California during the 1920s and 1930s worked in the professions for which they had prepared.

As a result, most Nisei — some of whom had college degrees and all of whom had been born in the United States — worked in Japanese shops, laundries, hotels, fruit stands, and produce stores. Those who worked as professionals, such as doctors and dentists, had only Japanese clients. Others became Japanese gardeners, even if they had no training in gardening. The Nisei were kept on the outside, and this angered many of them.

The second generation organized to fight back. They created Democratic Clubs throughout California to support legal changes to end discrimination. In 1930, they formed the Japanese American Citizens League, a civil rights group. Many were also active in the labor union movements of the 1930s.

Imprisonment for Being Japanese

World War II, during which the United States was pitted against Japan from 1941 to 1945, had a dramatic and in some cases devastating effect on Japanese American communities. Before the United States entered the war in 1941, Japantowns were thriving up and down the West Coast, filled with Japanese-speaking business people, Japanese-style housing, and Japanese community activities. But Japanese Americans were highly visible, first because of their race, second because of their language, third because of their geography, and, fourth, it would turn out, because Japan was at war with the United States. Perhaps inevitably,

In 1942, all West Coast Japanese had to evacuate their businesses and homes and report to prison camps. This Issei couple and their seven American-born children were considered "enemy aliens" when the United States went to war against Japan.

Japanese Americans on the West Coast were singled out as potential enemies of the United States.

In 1941, the Japanese military bombed U.S. naval forces at Pearl Harbor in Hawaii. In response, President Franklin D. Roosevelt declared war with Japan. The U.S. government also questioned the loyalty of Japanese Americans, treating them as if they were likely to help the Japanese government from within the United States. They were considered to be "enemy aliens" whose loyalty to the United States was suspect. Comparing the Nisei, who had been born as U.S. citizens, to baby snakes, one newspaper argued that snakes hatched from snake eggs are still snakes; they do not change their nature because of where they were born.

Government officials began rounding up Japanese Americans and sending them, without any trial, to internment camps, which were essentially a type of prison. These people had done nothing wrong. They were interned simply for having Japanese ancestry. Without a doubt, the underlying motivation of the internment was race: While Roosevelt signed the order to imprison the Japanese Americans, he argued against applying the same treatment to German and Italian Americans on the East Coast, immigrants and descendants from two nations that were also the enemy, but European.

In predominantly white California, more than 94,000 Japanese Americans were sent to internment camps for the duration of the war, which ended in 1945. Another 25,000 from the states of Washington and Oregon were interned as well. These 120,000 internees represented almost the entire West Coast population of Japanese Americans. Two-thirds of the internees were U.S. citizens by birth.

Because there were fewer Japanese Americans living in the interior states, their presence was seen as less threatening, and they were not imprisoned. Strangely enough, the Japanese Americans in Hawaii were not much affected by the war. Perhaps because, at the time, they represented 37 percent of the islands' population, they were regarded as "insiders" who belonged there.

Those headed for internment camps — almost the entire Japanese American mainland population — were forced to leave behind the property they had worked so hard to acquire. They were allowed to take along only bedding, personal articles, and eating utensils. Even infants were imprisoned, including a future U.S. representative, Robert Matsui of California.

Those who refused to cooperate were arrested, convicted, and sent to prison. Most, however, cooperated. They sold off their possessions, including ovens, cars, furniture, and houses. Mainstream Americans, knowing that the Japanese often had less than a week to sell everything, paid only tiny amounts for valuable household goods. Families were sent on trains and registered with numbers. Upon their arrival at the camps, they were surrounded by barbed wire and armed soldiers.

First the internees, or prisoners, were held temporarily at fairgrounds, racetracks, and stockyards that had been used for animal slaughter. Other prisoners lived in stables, sleeping in old flour sacks filled with straw. The housing was dirty, smelly, crowded, and noisy, without any quiet or privacy. Prisoners had to line up for mail, meals, showers, washrooms, laundry tubs, and movies. They were subjected to curfews and regular attendance checks. After a while, they were put on trains

again and sent to a more permanent location but not told where they were going.

The U.S. government established ten permanent internment camps. They were Topaz in Utah, Poston and Gila River in Arizona, Amache in Colorado, Jerome and Rohwer in Arkansas, Minidoka in Idaho, Manzanar and Tule Lake in California, and Heart Mountain in Wyoming. Most of the camps were located in isolated desert areas, without views of houses, trees, or green land. Everything was dusty and dry — sand filled the prisoners' mouths and nostrils.

In the camps, the prisoners lived in barracks, about 20 feet by 120 feet, divided into four or six rooms. Each family lived in one room, 20 feet by 20 feet, that contained a stove, a hanging bulb overhead, and one army cot and blanket apiece. The routine was strict: at 7:00 A.M., a blasting siren announced breakfast; the children went to school while the adults worked all day; then the internees ate in huge cafeterias at dinner time. People waited in long lines for food, and families could not eat together. Young couples worried about having children in the camp because they did not want their babies born as prisoners.

The adults, who were used to working for themselves as farmers and shopkeepers, were forced to work for the government for an hourly wage. They earned twelve dollars a month if unskilled, sixteen dollars if skilled, and nineteen if professionals. These wages were lower than they had been paid a half-century earlier in Hawaii. The work was tedious, and the prisoners soon became weakened, bored, and despairing. Some committed suicide.

Contributing to the War Effort

Young male internees who were eligible for military service were given a questionnaire to test their loyalty to the United States. But many, angry about the internment, answered "no" to virtually every question on the questionnaires; they were called "No, No Boys." The same spirit that caused the Nisei to form the Japanese American Citizens League (JACL) led some to fight back against injustice. They refused to declare loyalty to a country that treated them like "enemy aliens."

Some Japanese Americans, about thirty-three thousand in all, did join the war effort. The Nisei fighters translated Japanese documents and volunteered to fight in Japan. They spied on enemy commanders and reported secret communications. Others persuaded Japanese soldiers to surrender. They also fought bravely in Europe.

The internment of most West Coast Japanese Americans during World War II isolated Japanese Americans even from other Asian American groups. During the war, for example, Korean Americans wore tags saying, "I am a Korean, not Japanese," so that they would not experience the same discrimination the Japanese suffered.

As a result of their history in California, the heartbreak of the camps, and the loss of their property and dreams, many Issei and Nisei left the West Coast after the war. They resettled in cities such as Denver, Salt Lake City, and Chicago. This suited the government just fine; Japanese Americans would be so disbursed across the nation that they would not pose a threat to mainstream Americans. Although some communities, such as San Jose, California, welcomed their returning Japanese families, others made their hostility clear. Some local California train stations, for example, posted signed saying, "No Japs Allowed," and "No Japs Welcome." Japanese Americans' houses had been damaged or ruined, and many former internees were so old, ill, or broken-hearted that they simply resettled elsewhere.

Japanese American soldiers begin their military training in Mississippi during World War II. Eager to prove their loyalty, many young men volunteered to fight while still in the internment camps.

WORLD WAR II HEROISM

During World War II, while their relatives were imprisoned in camps, many Nisei volunteered to fight for the U.S. in order to prove their loyalty in the conflict against Japan. Thirty-three thousand Nisei served in battles and in military intelligence operations. On the Pacific front, several thousand served as interpreters and translators who deciphered Japanese battle plans, lists of ships, and secret codes.

For example, U.S. tanks were able to ambush Japanese invaders at Bataan because Richard Sakakida's translation revealed the Japanese battle plans. In Burma, Nisei soldiers crawled up to Japanese officers' quarters and translated their commands to the U.S. forces. They tapped phone lines, listened to radio reports, and translated field orders. In Okinawa, Japanese Americans explained to Okinawans that U.S. forces would not harm them, encouraging many Japanese to surrender. One U.S. general, the chief of intelligence in the Pacific, estimated that Nisei efforts shortened the war by two years.

In Europe, when the Nisei 100th Batallion merged with the 442nd Regiment, made up of Hawaiian and mainland Nisei, they lost more than one-fourth of the regiment fighting in Italy. In France, the troops fought the Germans hand-to-hand. In their efforts to save the Texan "Lost Battalion," 211 men surrounded by German troops, the 442nd suffered eight hundred casualties. Some Texans who were rescued burst out crying at the sight of the Japanese Americans. The 442nd was awarded more than eighteen thousand individual medals for outstanding service, including a Congressional Medal of Honor, Distinguished Service Crosses, Silver Stars, Bronze Stars, and Purple Hearts. Their bravery earned them a proud welcome from President Harry Truman — even though they still could not get a haircut at most California barbershops.

After the Internment

During the late1940s, many laws permitting discrimination were changed, thanks in part to the efforts of the Japanese American Citizens League (JACL), which fought hard to remind mainstream voters of Japanese American contributions, loyalty, and bravery during wartime. In the early 1950s, the Alien Land Law was revoked, permitting Japanese-born Americans to own their homes and farms. The law against mixed-race marriage was struck down. Most importantly, the 1952 McCarran-Walter Act allowed nonwhite immigrants to become citizens. The JACL had lobbied hard for the passage of that Act. Elderly Issei studied to become citizens.

Many Japanese Americans felt deeply ashamed of the internment, as if it had been their fault. They felt unsafe revealing their culture to mainstream Americans, so they moved to different communities, tried to blend in, and sometimes abandoned their culture.

Others, however, became so angry at their mistreatment that they began to fight. The organizations that remained, such as the JACL, became fighting machines. While their parents were dispirited, many Nisei developed a life-long dedication to civil rights and their Japanese heritage. The many achievements of the JACL included its support for the American civil rights movement, the movement that effectively brought African Americans the right to vote. The JACL, widely known for its focus and effectiveness, takes pride in being the oldest civil rights organization in the United States.

This mother and her daughter share a smile as they read together. Today's Japanese American families are diverse; some are headed by single parents, and others are blended families, with members from different cultures and ethnic groups.

CHAPTER THREE

FAMILY AND COMMUNITY
ENTERING THE MAINSTREAM

Although there is no "typical" Japanese American family, the Yamanaka family has many things in common with other Japanese American families today. The Yamanaka family is made up of a Japanese American man married to a mainstream American woman and their two children. The family lives far from his parents. The Yamanaka household is very democratic; every person has a right to be heard. They attend a traditional Presbyterian church in the suburbs, but they visit the local Buddhist temple a few times a year so that their children can attend Japanese festi-

vals. Japanese dolls and paintings decorate their home, but no Japanese is spoken there. Today's Japanese American family could not be more different than the typical Issei, or first-generation immigrant, family. Yet most share the goals and ambitions of any other mainstream American family.

The Family Today

Thoroughly American. As Chapter Two discussed, today's Japanese American population is part of the American mainstream for a number of reasons. Many of the Japanese

These Japanese American boys enjoy refreshing shaved ice cones in Hawaii. Japanese Americans are more numerous in Hawaii than anywhere else in the United States.

Americans living in the United States today are *Sansei,* the third generation, or their fourth-generation children, called *Yonsei.* The American-born internment survivors of the elder generation are grandparents now. The third-generation Sansei see themselves as American and act it. In high school and college, Sansei participate in student politics and athletics and have more non-Japanese than Japanese friends. After school, many marry non-Japanese. They do not seem, on the surface, to retain many Japanese cultural traits.

Yet even among Sansei families, some Japanese cultural characteristics remain. For example, Sansei mothers combine both Japanese and American styles of child rearing. One traditional Japanese value is that the strongest emotional bond is between a mother and her child. In the old style, children slept together, regardless of gender, and often their mother slept with them. Infants were coddled and pampered, so that they would become extremely close to their mother and therefore trusting of others. Even today, Sansei mothers sing to, carry, and play with their babies more than do most mainstream American mothers, who often expect their babies to learn to play by themselves and become independent early. As a result, many Japanese American babies spend less time alone than do most mainstream American babies.

Some Sansei feel more Japanese during traditional holidays, such as New Year's, when they may visit their parents and eat traditional food. They may still feel strong gratitude toward their parents, unlike some mainstream Americans, for the sacrifices made to raise and educate them. Gratitude and respect for parents is a strong Japanese, and East Asian, value. As they learn what their parents endured in the internment camps, many Sansei feel humbled and more grateful to their parents. As a result, many Sansei feel obligated to please their parents; they seek to fulfill their parents' expectations and make them happy. If they do not succeed, they may feel guilty and worried.

RAISING CHILDREN JAPANESE STYLE IN THE STATES

In the early decades of the 1900s, the Japanese gave up on the idea of legally becoming U.S. citizens because of laws against non-whites becoming citizens of the United States. But in their efforts to become good U.S. residents, some Japanese adopted American customs. They took Sundays off from work, like American Christians. During Prohibition (the period in the 1920s when selling alcohol was illegal in the United States), they tried to avoid drinking. They also tried to adopt some American methods of raising their children.

In his history of Asian Americans, *Strangers from a Different Shore,* Ronald Takaki, an Issei, creates a vivid portrait of the cultural conflicts faced by Japanese Americans. In one instance, many women, who were used to working in the fields with their babies strapped to their backs, began to wonder about the impression that this practice might make on other Americans.

To a Japanese woman, this custom might have meant that she does not want her children to have much freedom; or it might mean that she gives her children lots of love by keeping them so close. In fact, the reaction that most Japanese Americans encountered from other Americans was criticism and resentment for working so hard that they needed to take their children with them.

Traditional Values. Despite their American experiences, many Sansei still identify themselves as Japanese, or Japanese American. A strong majority of Sansei women in California, for example, eat Japanese food regularly, favor Japanese art, and think about their Japanese identity. Many have attended Japanese American theater. Furthermore, they usually feel strongly obligated to repay a favor or a gift.

According to Japanese custom, gifts or favors are carefully remembered so that each person repays what he or she is given. Especially within the Japanese family, circle of friends, or community, this custom survives. Some Sansei women complain that this obligation limits free expression, yet others see it as a valuable way to build relationships. Nurturing relationships among relatives, within the community, and with other friends remains a powerful traditional custom among many Japanese Americans. This is especially true in families that carry on the tradition of respect for one's elders. If the young people were to forget a gift, their parents might feel ashamed.

Other traditional Japanese values, however, are rarely followed among today's Japanese American families. In more traditional families, for example, each family member has a role to play, and some roles are more important than others. In older Japanese American families, the father had strong authority over other family members. The first son supported the parents and had more privileges than the second son. Older people were due more respect than younger people, and males had more privileges than females. The Japanese language requires the speaker to address people either as above, below, or equal in rank. Yet as Japanese Americans have adapted to the more democratic American family style, most of these values have faded. Respect for the elderly, however, remains important.

GENERATION NAMES: ISSEI, NISEI, SANSEI, YONSEI

Issei were born in Japan. They are first-generation Japanese Americans. The Issei mostly farmed on the West Coast. This generation lost everything in the internment. Most of the Issei have died.

Nisei are the children of the Issei. They are second-generation Japanese Americans. Many Nisei went with their parents to the internment camps. Some were born in the camps. The Nisei are now grandparents. They still make many of the decisions in the Japanese American community.

Sansei are the children of Nisei and the grandchildren of immigrant Issei. Thus, they are third-generation Japanese Americans. Many Sansei are from families that have been in the United States for as long as or longer than families of European Americans. Some Sansei have inherited their parents' pride in their Japanese ancestry. They may live or work in the Japanese American community.

Yonsei are fourth-generation Japanese Americans. Most do not speak Japanese.

Other Groups:

Kibei were born in the United States and sent back to Japan for their education. Most Kibei are Nisei.

Yobiyose were a small group of Japanese who were asked to come to the United States by elderly Issei relatives.

Care for the Elderly

Traditionally, the needs and values of the family were more important than those of any individual in it. Personal relationships, including marriages, were arranged to benefit the household, rather than to satisfy personal desire. Loyalty, obedience, and controlled behavior enabled family members to protect what the Japanese call the "house." Every family member, with the exception of daughters who married, remained close from birth until death. For example, many members of the first generation of Japanese American elderly saw their children and grandchildren daily. Earlier in this century, about half the elderly Issei lived with their children, and of those, about two-thirds lived with their sons, according to tradition.

Yet because the Japanese American family has blended so much into mainstream culture, the custom of living with elderly parents has faded away. Older Japanese Americans now often live far from their families. But respect for the elderly survives, especially among the second-generation Nisei. So organizations led by Nisei have taken over this traditional family responsibility. The community has formed its own nursing homes and community centers that house and nurture their elders.

In Chicago, for example, a community service group has built a retirement and nursing home for Japanese American elderly. Because the Japanese American community created it, the nursing home is sensitive to the needs of traditional Japanese Americans. Staff members speak Japanese and celebrate Japanese holidays. Japanese food is served at mealtime, and the dining room is decorated with Japanese artwork. Ministers and priests conduct Buddhist as well as Christian services. Japanese music is played in common areas, and a traditional garden lies outside the building. The very name of the home, Keiro, means respect for the elderly.

The organization that built the nursing home is called the Japanese American Service Committee (JASC). The JASC provides many services, including adult day care, Meals on Wheels (delivery of meals to home-

A grandmother in Hawaiian flowers poses in front of her collection of family pictures. Even first-generation immigrants adapt to the cultures of their adopted homes.

bound people), and housecleaning and nursing programs. Many of the people served by the JASC are not Japanese American — they just happen to live in the communities that used to be Japantowns. In one city, the JASC also provides services to Latinos and African Americans.

The End of Japantowns

As a result of the World War II internment, the Japantowns on the West Coast were almost eliminated. Many Japanese were afraid to return to what used to be home, so they spread out into smaller communities throughout the United States. West Coast Japantowns became smaller and more discreet, but they have rebounded since the war. And although Japantowns sprang up in cities in the U.S. interior, most residents moved away to mainstream communities as soon as possible. Many Japanese Americans now live in the suburbs and travel to Japantown only for shopping, worship, or special events. As the elder generation passed away and the second-generation Nisei, many of whom did not speak fluent Japanese, took over, the Japantowns lost vitality. Virtually no new immigrants arrived to refresh these communities.

In many cities, the JASC, Buddhist temples or Japanese Christian churches, the Japanese American Civic League, and a few Japanese restaurants are all that is left of a traditional Japantown. And many of the Japanese restaurants are run by non-Japanese immigrants, such as Koreans. In most cities, these organizations are spread out over wide geographic areas. In fact, in every U.S. city except on the

This tea garden in San Francisco shows the influence of Japanese culture. San Francisco has been the home of a strong Japanese American community since before 1900.

West Coast and in Hawaii, Japantown has all but disappeared.

Like many other ethnic groups, the Japanese Americans have assimilated into U.S. culture. Unlike many other groups, however, they were forced to. Yet with strong spirits and pride in their heritage, many Japanese Americans still serve and try to hold on to their community.

The JASC, which is active in many cities, supports the Japanese American community through activities and fund-raising. In the past, activities such as picnics and athletic contests held the Nisei community together. Now, however, as the Nisei generation ages, these activities take place less often. Members of the third-generation Sansei, now in their thirties and forties and parents themselves, are ready to take over and lead the community.

Since many Sansei grew up in mainstream communities as minorities but speaking no Japanese, they struggle over passing their heritage on to their children. Some just do not feel Japanese and do not think about their heritage. Others work hard to bring their community's history and culture to the youngest Japanese Americans.

These Sansei may attend the JASC fundraising activities or even organize them. They may bring their children to Buddhist temples — if not for religious services, then for cultural activities. These include Japanese language schools, drum or tea-ceremony lessons, or festivals. One activist even started a publishing company in order to keep alive Asian American children's stories. Other Sansei strengthen the community by running shelters for battered Asian American women and children, providing free legal services, or arguing for better political representation for all Asian Americans. Despite these and other expressions of cultural and community solidarity, however, the internment took a great cultural toll on Japanese Americans. Most of them drove their ethnic pride underground, almost hiding their heritage. As a result, those today who want to claim their history and role in U.S. society must struggle to do so.

The Exceptions: Hawaii and California

The lives of most Japanese Americans living in Hawaii and California are radically different than those in the rest of the United States. In Hawaii, where Japanese Americans were the majority of the population even just

JAPANESE NATIONALS: A SEPARATE COMMUNITY

Hundreds and thousands of Japanese nationals — that is, people who are citizens of Japan — live in major U.S. cities during work assignments for Japanese companies. Surprisingly, these Japanese nationals have little or no contact with Japanese Americans. They remain in separate communities for the duration of their stay.

In Chicago, for example, children of Japanese nationals attend a separate school. It is staffed by Japanese-trained teachers and follows a Japanese curriculum. Many families attend a separate Japanese Christian church in a northern suburb; they are rarely seen at the local Japanese American Christian churches or Buddhist temples. A special suburban market caters to them, selling fresh (and expensive) seafood, vegetables, and ceramics. This market has become popular among Asian Americans of all types who appreciate Asian merchandise. At the market, departing Japanese executives advertise "gently used" luxury cars for sale at bargain prices as they prepare to return to their native land.

The families of these Japanese nationals consist almost without exception of executive fathers, stay-at-home mothers, and their children. These families keep to themselves, separate from the rest of society. If their children were to become Americanized, their parents fear, they would never fit in with the culture at home. By attending separate churches, schools, and even markets, Japanese nationals successfully preserve their distinct values.

after the war, Japantowns were everywhere. A Japanese American in Hawaii, if challenged by someone who was Caucasian, could feel enough confidence to confront the person directly. Their numbers provided strength and opportunity. Furthermore, Hawaiian Japanese Americans were not interned during the war, so their culture was not weakened. It thrives to this day.

Los Angeles and San Francisco also have dynamic Japantowns, where virtually all the businesses, restaurants, architecture, and residents are still Japanese. Their Japanese-language newspapers publish more often than papers do in other communities. Young activists meet together and plan ways to strengthen the bonds among Japanese Americans. Other communities recognize their culture. Because of their greater numbers, longer history, and vibrant cultural heritage, West Coast Japanese Americans still have a place to call home.

The Byodo-In Temple in Oahu, Hawaii, is modeled after an original in Japan. One of the first things immigrant plantation laborers did was to build temples and sponsor the immigration of Buddhist priests.

Japanese American Civic League and the Redress Movement

One organization that has helped Japanese Americans find their strength and identity since the internment is the Japanese American Civic League (JACL). During the 1970s, many members of the Nisei generation, having finished raising their families and establishing their careers, found time to reflect on the wrongs that had been done to their community during World War II. A number of activists, sponsored by the JACL, decided to press for redress, or a remedy, from the U.S. government.

As a result of their activism, the government admitted that the imprisonment had been unjust. In 1988, the Civil Liberties Act guaranteed payment to every American of Japanese descent whose family members had been wrongly imprisoned during the war. The Japanese American community had taken a wrong and made it right by refusing to accept injustice, demanding proof of apology, and creating an example for other minorities to stand up for their individual rights as fully enfranchised Americans. Despite the absence of Japantowns and other geographical neighborhoods, the Japanese American community has reconfirmed its identity and dignity.

43

Wearing a traditional Japanese kimono, this woman prepares for her wedding. Such customs have all but disappeared in mainland U.S. Japanese communities.

CHAPTER FOUR

RELIGION AND CELEBRATIONS
A MELLOW BLEND OF FAITHS

One summer Sunday, the Yamada family is very busy. In the morning, this Japanese American family attends a Unitarian religious service. Because their mother is Jewish and their father's family is Buddhist and Christian, they have found a home in the open-minded Unitarian Church. In Sunday school, the Yamada children study Jesus' Sermon on the Mount. After returning home for a quick lunch of sandwiches, the Yamadas pack up the car again and drive to the Buddhist temple. It is Bon Odori, the summer festival of dance, parades, and celebration. The Yamada kids love this festival. They get to eat Japanese foods, play, and make origami, or folded paper, figures. Even though the children speak no Japanese, the adults make everyone feel special.

The Japanese are open to many religious traditions, and so are Japanese Americans. When the Issei, or first generation of Japanese Americans, migrated to the United States, they brought Buddhism with them, while holding on to some customs of Shinto, the original religion of Japan. As groups of Japanese Americans became established in California and Hawaii, many communities built humble temples and invited Buddhist ministers over from Japan. Japanese American Buddhism, however, like other Japanese traditions, was weakened by the experience of the internment of Japanese Americans during World War II. And Shinto, a collection of ancient, nature-based customs, has all but disappeared from Japanese American culture.

SHINTO CUSTOMS

Shinto, Japan's ancient, native religion, is based on nature. It is still seen in cultural rituals among Japanese today. Many Japanese Americans do not even know that some of their family customs originated in Shinto. In ancient times, the Japanese worshiped farming, the earth, and ancestor gods. By the fourth century A.D., every family had its own special god in whose honor the family would build a shrine. Some Shinto customs include visiting shrines at New Year's, participating in shrine festivals, praying to Shinto gods for success on school tests, and taking children to be blessed by Shinto gods. Because Shinto is tied to the earth, growth, and the home, most Japanese weddings are done in the Shinto style. The first generation of Japanese immigrants relied on some Shinto rituals, but today most Japanese Americans would have trouble recognizing them.

After the 1940s, when Japanese Americans began assimilating increasingly into American culture, many Nisei, or second-generation Japanese Americans, gave up their distinctive religious roots and joined mainstream churches. As a result, many Japanese Americans today participate in mainstream Christian worship throughout American cities and suburbs. Some

A traditional Shinto shrine at a New Year's celebration in Hawaii. Although Shinto is rarely practiced in the United States today, many of its customs and rituals have influenced the family practices of contemporary Japanese Americans.

Japanese traditions persist, though, in Japanese Christian churches and in the Japanese Buddhist temples, which are usually found in the nation's larger cities. In these institutions, Japanese culture is passed on through the third and fourth generation. Furthermore, some Japanese Americans have rejoined their ancestors' faiths in an effort to reconnect with their heritage.

Buddhism

Buddhism came to Japan in the fifth century A.D. By the end of the sixth century, it had become Japan's official faith. Some of

Japan's oldest remaining buildings are ancient Buddhist temples. During the Edo Period, from the 1600s to the mid-1800s, all families were required to register at one of the country's Buddhist temples. At the time that most Japanese emigrated to the United States, Japan was overwhelmingly Buddhist. Most Issei were Buddhist, and many raised their children, the Nisei generation, in their traditional faith. In Hawaii, Japanese laborers built Buddhist temples in order to support their growing community. Many Japanese Buddhist temples sprang up throughout California and the West Coast, where Japanese Americans had businesses, farms, and schools. The temple schools taught Japanese language and customs to the Nisei, and immigrant families attended worship services and community meetings together at the temples.

After Japanese Americans left the internment camps where they had been imprisoned during World War II, they moved into many different communities throughout the United States. To avoid unwanted attention, many joined mainstream Christian churches, where often they were the only members of Japanese descent.

At the same time, in cities throughout the United States, groups of Japanese Americans formed Japantowns for community and cultural support. In these Japantowns, Japanese Buddhist temples as well as Japanese Christian congregations were born. As on the West Coast, these Japanese American religious groups taught cultural traditions as well. One of these traditional Japanese rituals is the Buddhist funeral.

THE BUDDHA AND HIS PHILOSOPHY

The Buddha was born Siddhartha Gautama about twenty-five hundred years ago in northern India. Although he was a prince with many talents, he left his father's palace on a spiritual quest in his late twenties. He wandered through the country seeking knowledge, but he was unsatisfied. One day, he sat under a tree and meditated. As a result of his inward search, he found truth and attained self-awareness. Eventually, he became known as the Buddha. He was not, and is not, a god. For the rest of his forty-five years on earth, he taught his way of life.

Unlike Christianity, Buddhism has no missionary spirit; it does not seek to convert anyone. The religion holds that each individual must seek, learn, and live his or her own life. Because of its respect for the individual, Buddhism rejects separating people according to class, race, and religion.

Buddhist Funerals. The Buddhist tradition is to hold a wake and then a funeral at which family, relatives, and friends mourn by the coffin. The wake begins with the preparation of a funeral altar by the mortician. A Buddhist priest chants texts known as sutras, gives the deceased a Buddhist name, and burns incense. The priest gives a short talk about the deceased during the funeral, which can have an open or closed casket. After the service, family members take guests out for a meal. There they share memories of the deceased, celebrate his or her life, and provide hospitality.

Some mourners accompany the casket to a crematorium. Unlike the custom in Japan,

A tall marker shows where a Japanese American has been buried. Japanese-style graveyards are common in Hawaii and on the West Coast.

however, the mourners do not stay while the body is burned. After the cremation, the remains are returned to the temple for a period of thirty days, where the spirit is purified before the ashes are buried.

A short burial service follows. At the service, an urn chosen by the family and containing the deceased's ashes is buried in a small cement vault. In Japan, one vault contains the remains of an entire family, but in the United States, where there is more land, family members usually have their own small plot. A headstone gives the deceased's name and birth and death dates. In some West Coast cities, where the Japanese American community is large, there are separate Japanese American cemeteries. Other cities may have separate Japanese sections, or individuals may just buy plots in mainstream cemeteries.

One Buddhist Temple. In the typical Buddhist temple, most of the members are Japanese American, although a few are Caucasian or Chinese American. The majority of members are second-generation Nisei. Some are Sansei, or third generation. When the children of the Sansei are old enough to attend Sunday school, some return to the temples of their parents, but their numbers are small. The temple is most often located in a neighborhood with a fairly high crime rate, and Sansei living in the suburbs often fear returning to the old neighborhood.

No one is required to attend temple services. All people are welcome, and there are no formal membership requirements. Each Sunday begins with a fellowship meditation which lasts from 9:30 to 10:30 A.M. After removing their shoes, individuals enter a meditation room where they sit, cross-legged, facing the room's center. The room is quiet, clean, and decorated in a simple manner. Light is provided by slightly open screened windows.

A boy stands before the altar of a Zen Buddhist temple. Zen is one of the many sects, or groups, of Buddhism, the most common religion among early Japanese Americans.

An altar stands in the room's center; at the altar are a statue of the Buddha, a vase of flowers, burning incense, and a lit candle.

The goal of meditation is to quiet the mind and to find calm. This allows the Buddhist to see reality clearly. As a result, the process of meditation in this temple follows simple steps. At the sound of wooden clappers, meditators press their palms together in a show of respect, which is called *Gassho*. The sound of a bell signals the beginning of the meditation period, during which individuals sit without moving or making noise. During meditation, meditators reflect on their lives and seek to see things clearly. At the end of the sitting period, the clappers are struck again, and meditators do Gassho and relax their legs. Following the meditation period, a light breakfast of fresh fruit, toast, and tea is served.

Following the morning meditation is the temple's regular Sunday service, which begins at 11:00 A.M. and lasts about forty-five minutes. At first a gong is struck, and people rise to sing. After reading a chant, people listen to

BUDDHIST SYMBOLS

Statues of the Buddha: A statue of the Buddha represents a man sitting with legs crossed, hands touching in his lap, and eyes closed. He is sitting in the lotus position for meditation. Buddha was a man who achieved enlightenment. The statues are not worshiped; instead, they represent a goal for Buddhists to achieve.

Flowers: Flowers symbolize how things change in life. Beautiful in the morning, many fade by afternoon. Humans are faced with old age, sickness, and death, and flowers' short lives remind us of these facts. Nevertheless, we appreciate flowers because of their beauty, just as Buddhists seek to appreciate the beauty of life on a daily basis.

Incense: Incense used in a temple may be powdered, or it may come in sticks or cakes of different shapes. Its colors may be purple, black, yellow, green, or brown. But its symbolism is always the same: A Buddhist's goal is to spread sweetness, like a fragrance, to others through helpfulness and friendliness.

Candlelight: Candlelight symbolizes wisdom. Without light, our physical world is so dark that we see nothing. In the spiritu- al world, wisdom is the light that allows us to see. Wisdom, unlike knowledge, is gained through direct experience and reflection.

Gongs: Gongs are used in Buddhist temples and homes. They announce a meeting or different parts of a service. In addition, they serve as a symbol, helping worshipers to meditate. Their beautiful sound gives the person something to focus on in meditation.

Gassho: Gassho is the placing of the palms of the hands together in front of the heart and then bowing. It symbolizes respect. One palm represents the worshiper; the other, pressed tightly to it, represents the object. The object may be the Buddha or another person.

Meditation Beads: Beads, each representing an individual, are linked together on a string to symbolize unity and harmony. Each bead is connected with all the others and cannot exist alone. Meditation beads are used when doing Gassho, but they are merely a symbol, not prayer beads. There is no prayer in Buddhism, which does not believe in a supreme being who can hear and answer prayers.

the teachings of the reverend, who discusses individual experiences and points out errors or mistakes so that the listeners can learn from them. Then the group reads passages together and does Gassho.

Another talk follows, with the reverend standing on a raised platform in front of the altar. The altar is red, golden, and black and houses a statue of the Buddha. Candle-like lamps hang from either side of the altar, lighting up the statue. Following this second talk, the community sings again and listens to the reverend perform a formal chant. A hymn and voluntary donation follow. Then the reverend closes the service with announcements about temple groups.

Members and their children can participate in the community at every step of their lives. In the Infant's First Service (Hatsu Mairi), held every May, members' babies are formally presented to the community for the first time. Some temples also have a play group for toddlers that meets once a month. Teenagers can attend a Dharma school, which teaches Buddhist traditions, Japanese language, and Japanese culture. As adults, members who seek to follow seriously the Buddhist path are given a Buddhist name in the Three Treasures (Ti Sarana) ceremony, which takes place in March and September. Through the Dharma school, cultural celebrations, and lessons in Japanese language and culture, the Buddhist temple serves an important role in preserving Japanese American culture.

Christianity

Because Christian missionaries were active in Japan during the Meiji Period (between 1868 and 1912), Christianity had a great effect on the first generation of Japanese Americans, the Issei. For example, Christian missionaries opened many schools for girls and educated future picture brides, who would travel to the United States for arranged marriages. Yet because Christianity was banned in Japan for centuries, most Issei were not Christian. In fact, one Issei who wrote about being Christian in Japan said that her family was discriminated against because of their faith. Their father, a doctor, could not get patients, and other villagers threw garbage at their house. Such persecution in Japan is now a thing of the past. Today there are many Japanese American Christians.

Japanese Christian Churches. During and immediately after World War II, Japanese Americans were prohibited by law from forming their own religious congregations. They were expected to assimilate into mainstream American churches, and many did. Some mainstream churches defied the law, however, and offered space to Issei ministers, who formed Japanese Christian groups. Today in the United States, Japanese Christian churches may be found in many major cities. Some cities even have different denominations of Japanese Christian churches, such as Presbyterian and United Church of Christ.

At first, these congregations were made up of Issei and their children, but as the Issei passed away, many Nisei stopped attending the churches. Attendance fell away as Japanese Americans blended into mainstream culture. Some churches had to sell their buildings and rent space from other congregations. Yet as the Sansei, or third generation, began to have children, the popularity of Japanese American congregations began to increase once again. Many parents feel that Japanese American churches and temples provide for cultural continuity and that church is the only place their children can meet Japanese Americans and other Asians. The churches have begun to reach out to these assimilated Americans.

A blended Japanese American family worships in Chicago's Lakeview Japanese Christian Church. The grandmother escaped the internment camps by leaving California, and her family settled in the Midwest. Many Japanese Americans have adopted Christianity as their faith.

A Typical Japanese American Christian Church. In many churches, weekly services in Japanese for Issei and Japanese nationals follow English-speaking services. Celebrations allow the two groups to blend and share cultural traditions. Older members may bring traditional Japanese dishes to Easter, Thanksgiving, and Mother's Day celebrations. The third generation thus gets an opportunity to learn about their heritage because, for the most part, the Nisei do not speak Japanese at home, and often they will not discuss their wartime experiences. In this relaxed group setting, however, the young or new Issei and some Nisei will teach the third generation about their heritage and experiences.

Sunday school for the children takes place while the English service is being conducted. Sometimes, the children sing songs during the adult service at Christmas and other holidays or sing special hymns in Japanese. Sunday school members may go caroling at Japanese nursing homes during the Christmas season. Some teachers may bring Japanese treats, such as rice crackers, for their students. Other teachers try to blend their discussions of Christianity with discussions about being Japanese American.

One teacher, for example, used as a cultural lesson the story of Jesus meeting the Samaritan woman at the well. Jesus did this even though at that time there were taboos against Jews speaking to Samaritans and men speaking to women. After the story, the teacher asked the children if they ever felt as if they were different or as if they did not fit in. Some children admitted that people thought they were different because they looked Asian. Then the children discussed how Jesus would want them to treat other people who looked different. In another lesson, the teacher showed the children Hebrew characters, like those in which the Bible was originally written. Then she showed children characters in Japanese and Chinese. This comparison helped make foreign languages acceptable and special to the children.

Some Japanese Christian churches blend Eastern and Western traditions every week. In fact, some are international. These churches include among their members other Asian Americans, immigrants from non-Asian countries, and even mainstream Americans. By celebrating Easter and Christmas and teaching Bible stories, these churches often resemble mainstream American congregations. The Buddhist temples are often more culturally Japanese, incorporating Japanese festivals that include wearing costumes and kimonos, performing traditional dances, and teaching Japanese crafts.

Matsuri: Ceremonies Based on Nature, Life, and Death

In Japan, festivals — or *Matsuri* — take place almost daily, but each community, generation, and religion celebrates in its own style. Partly because the Japanese American community spread out after the internment, a certain ceremony may be observed in only one city or even in only one temple. Celebrations such as Japan Day and the Emperor's Birthday are no longer even held in the United States. Associations for Japanese Americans who come from particular regions in Japan celebrate their own events. These include church bazaars, community festivals, and big commercial festivities. In Los Angeles, for example, there is an entire week devoted to the Nisei, or the second generation. San Francisco has an autumn festival. Although different communities hold different celebrations, several celebrations are familiar to most Japanese

Americans. These include New Year's, Children's Days, Star Festival, and the Bon Dance.

New Year's: Shogatsu. New Year's Day is a very special occasion for most Japanese Americans. Families toast the new year with rice wine and eat a traditional soup with steamed, pounded, sticky rice — called *mochi* — in it. Sometimes families visit relatives and close friends to wish them a good year or prepare to receive visitors themselves. At each home, families share greetings, enjoy food and drink, and relax together. The food is important. A boiled vegetable dish must be served, along with tempura (deep fried shrimp and vegetables), sushi (raw fish rolls), and teriyaki (marinated meat, chicken, or fish). Traditional Japanese Americans eat buckwheat noodles to symbolize long life and continuity across the years. Today, some Japanese Americans have added traditional American holiday foods, such as ham, turkey, and even Chinese food.

Other traditional customs that are sometimes observed by Japanese Americans include cleaning house for the beginning of the new year, praying for good fortune, and paying off debts. Children sometimes fly kites, spin tops, and receive small gifts of money from parents and relatives. They do origami, which is folding paper into special shapes, such as a crane, which is a symbol of long life.

Hina Matsuri. Hina Matsuri, celebrated on March 3, is now known as the Doll Festival. Hina Matsuri is a holiday for girls. Traditionally on Hina Matsuri, girls pray for a good marriage, eat treats, and set out dolls in fancy dress on decorated platforms. In traditional Japan, dolls were part of a girl's wedding riches or dowry. As a result, dolls are not played with the way they are in the United States. During the festival, girls wear kimonos and serve tea cakes, rice wine, and special rice to honor their dolls.

The dolls are made to resemble both adults and children. Most are made of ceramic and cloth, although some are made of paper and wood. Usually, fifteen dolls are displayed on a special structure with several levels and covered with a bright red cloth that symbolizes the sun, liveliness, and good fortune. The main dolls, known as Court people, are used to symbolize the Emperor and Empress. Often Japanese American girls display Japanese-style dolls. However, they may also display their American-style dolls; instead of dressing traditionally or serving special foods, they dress in their nicest American clothing and eat their favorite American treats.

Children's Day. Children's Day, or Tango no Sekku, was traditionally for boys, but it is now renamed to include all children. It takes place on May 5. Traditionally, parents would buy their sons samurai dolls and mini helmets and pray for their sons' success in life. In the past on this day, families used to gather herbs and symbolic plants, such as iris leaves. Iris symbolizes uprightness and a military spirit, so the paper helmets, even today, are decorated with iris leaves. Boys may also fly colorful, long fish kites in their yards.

Children's Day became popular during the Meiji Period, during which many Japanese left for the United States, and so it is often celebrated here today. Now, Japanese American sweet shops make special foods, such as a sweet rice cake wrapped in bamboo, which symbolizes constancy and devotion. Another cake, filled with sweet bean, is wrapped in oak leaf, which symbolizes strength and protectiveness.

Tanabata. Tanabata is traditionally celebrated on July 7. It became popular in Japan during the Edo Era (1603-1868), just prior to the time when most Japanese Americans emigrated from Japan. It is sometimes known as the Weaving Loom Festival, or the Star Festi-

Carp windsock kites fly on May 5, which is Children's Day. Traditional festivals are celebrated in many Japanese American communities.

val, because it is based on a myth about two stars in the Northern Hemisphere. According to Chinese legend, the weaver star, which was a woman, fell in love with the herder star, which was a man. The weaver and the herder stars were so busy planning their wedding that they neglected their work. As punishment, the king (the weaver's father) separated the two on opposite sides of the heavens. When the weaver pleaded to see her lover, her father agreed that she could only see him once a year, on the seventh day of the seventh lunar month.

In the United States, July 7 celebrations of Tanabata are usually limited to small groups of people celebrating the two stars' meeting with poetry readings. Throughout this country, however, more communities are celebrating Tanabata with traditional exhibits, such as those seen in Japan.

Tanabata decorations include the symbols of poetry, weaving, or other forms of good luck, which hang from tree branches or bamboo trees. Strips of paper or strips of colored cloth display love poetry or weaving. Other symbols that hang from branches in Tanabata displays include a crane for long life, a brush for beautiful calligraphy (writing), a net for hunting well, a lottery basket for good luck, a kimono for protection, and a money pouch for saving.

Bon Odori. Bon Odori is a festival of dancing, celebrations, and parades that is held at many Buddhist temples during July and August. Traditionally, it was part of a three-day Buddhist festival to express gratitude. Relatives of those recently dead would dance and sing to please their ancestors' spirits. During this festival, Buddhists place offerings on small

Three women dance in Okinawan costumes. Although Japanese Americans no longer wear kimonos, many remain proud of their cultural heritage and study traditional dances.

altars. Standing on high platforms, musicians play flutes and drums, making melodies for people to perform special dances.

In Japan, Bon Odori became an expression of feelings through dance, and the dances often reflected each region's unique style. In the United States, these regional styles have carried over into Japanese American culture. In general, dancers in tradional summer kimonos dance in a circle around a drum raised up on a platform. Different objects, such as round fans, hand towels, and hand clackers, are used in different dances. Although some dancers practice for weeks in advance, many unrehearsed dancers just join in. In cities such as San Francisco and Los Angeles, Bon Odori is celebrated in big parades with professional dancers.

A California girl dances with a fan at the summer Bon Odori festival. Japanese American children learn these customs from grandparents, Japanese cultural centers, or Buddhist temples.

Keeping a Culture Alive. During the internment and afterward, the Japanese American community lost much of its power, language, and religious tradition. When the Japanese American population spread throughout the United States in the 1940s and 1950s, dozens of Japanese American communities had to rebuild their heritage while individuals rebuilt their lives. Traditions of religion, culture, and celebration were often put aside while second-generation members raised their young families. Nevertheless, Buddhist, Japanese Christian, and Matsuri traditions have survived. Now, third-generation members are visiting Buddhist temples, other Asian Americans attend Japanese Christian churches, and whole communities celebrate regional festivals. Despite their hardships, Japanese Americans appreciate their religious culture and are investing their time to make sure that it stays alive.

A Japanese American father serves *shirataki* noodles to his daughter. A traditional Japanese father would expect his wife to serve the food.

CHAPTER FIVE

CUSTOMS, EXPRESSIONS, AND HOSPITALITY
AN ARTFUL BLEND

Lisa Kumaki Jones had invited her friend, Josephine, for dinner Friday night. Her grandparents were coming over, and the family was going to eat Japanese style. But it had been a long time since her grandparents had visited; they lived far away, in Utah, and Lisa's lived in New York City. During the evening, Lisa forgot how to "act Japanese" and made some mistakes. Fortunately, her grandparents loved their granddaughter more than anything, so her mistakes were forgiven. The next day, however, her grandmother spent several hours teaching Lisa how to behave Japanese style.

Entering a Home

When the elder Kumakis entered their family's home, they immediately took off their shoes. Their daughter, Lisa's mother, had soft, embroidered slippers waiting for the old people to wear. When Lisa and Josephine arrived, however, they threw off their coats and kept on their shoes. In a Japanese-style home, people remove their shoes before entering the living area because people do not sit on raised furniture. They sit on mats on the floor where people walk.

Traditional Japanese Americans believe in treating the elderly with respect. When Lisa yelled, "Hey, Grandma!" Mrs. Kumaki, who was talking in the living room, became silent with shock. In traditional Japanese American culture, young people are not supposed to yell at their elders. Instead, their voices should be gentle and soft. Lisa smiled and hugged her grandparents, introducing Josephine to them. "Josephine, this is grandma and grandpa Kumaki," she said, smiling at everyone. Lisa's mother shook her head. "Introduce your grandparents first," she whispered to Lisa. As a sign of their social status, young people are presented to their elders.

Gift-giving is another important custom among Japanese Americans. Accordingly, Lisa's grandmother left a pile of gifts by the front door when she arrived. There were three: one for Lisa, one for her father, and one for her mother. Each gift was wrapped in white paper with a gold-and-red cord tied in a bow around it. The paper was folded crisply over the left side of the package. The gifts looked nothing like the gifts Lisa wrapped. Hers were wrinkly, the paper barely came together underneath the package, and she used a stick-on bow. She lifted the gift as if to open it, and her mother shook her head sharply, "No." Lisa frowned until she remembered something about waiting until the guests left before opening her gifts. She later learned that the custom of waiting to open gifts allows gift-givers to preserve their dignity if they cannot afford an expensive present.

After the girls got snacks in the kitchen, they joined their elders in the living room. Although the family had American-style couches and chairs, Lisa's mother had put out large,

GIFT GIVING

Traditional Japanese Americans bring a gift whenever they visit someone. Although it is important to offer a worthwhile gift, it is equally important to offer an appropriate gift. A gift that is too expensive may embarrass the recipient, who will then be required to return a gift of equal value sometime in the future. A small gift, carefully chosen and beautifully wrapped, is an important gesture of thoughtfulness and respect.

Gifts are offered for many occasions, including seasonal celebrations; to suit many moods, such as joy or sadness; and as an expression of sympathy, a thank you, or a farewell. For mid-year, gifts such as fans and lanterns are appropriate for hot weather. For year-end, including New Year's, good gifts include salmon, duck, or pheasant. Dolls are offered for Children's Days in May and March, and money is offered at funerals. In return for gifts, receivers may offer special rice cakes or small, beautiful pieces of silk cloth.

Gifts are wrapped with special care in Japanese culture. Special Japanese wrapping paper is made by hand. All gifts are wrapped in white paper and tied with a special paper cord. For formal gifts, two sheets of paper are used, whereas for simple or sad occasions, just one sheet is enough. The giver wraps the gift precisely, without wrinkles, and the paper is folded over the right-hand side of the package so that it meets along the left side of the package. Around the package is a knot with loops on the top that resemble the wings of a butterfly. For unhappy occasions, the paper is folded in the opposite direction, so that it meets on the right-hand side. The knotted cord may be red and white or gold and white for happy or regular events. Gold-and-silver cords are used only for weddings, when a more permanent-looking square knot is used.

Before offering the gift, the giver must write on the package. "Happiness" is used on some packages, and "to the spirit of the departed" is used on others. The giver's name is written at the bottom center. The receiver's name is at the upper left, like a letterhead. When a gift is offered, the recipient thanks the giver, bows, and then places the gift aside to be opened later. Opening a gift in the presence of the giver is considered bad manners; in case the gift is not appropriate, the giver might be embarrassed. Gifts are always acknowledged with a visit, a call, or a note of thanks.

Today's Japanese Americans, although perhaps more gracious or formal than many mainstream Americans, do not follow the same strict rules that their parents or grandparents might have. Upon arriving at a party, for example, they may offer flowers, a bottle of wine, or a token gift for the child of the house. A mainstream American who expects a young Japanese American to bring a doll or a game may be quite disappointed to receive the traditional gift of pickles, wrapped in crisp white paper.

square cushions for sitting on the floor. The girls each took one and sat down, cross-legged. Lisa's grandmother pursed her lips and said something to Lisa's mother in Japanese. Lisa found out later that girls were supposed to sit with their legs tucked underneath them, not crossed in front. Lisa's mother had never mentioned this custom, which was very traditional. At any rate, Lisa and Josephine soon tired of sitting on the floor. When it was time for dinner, they could not help rushing into the dining room and taking their seats.

A Japanese-Style Meal

On the table were traditional Japanese-style place settings. Small lacquered bowls filled with clear soybean-paste soup lay on the left. In the middle was a small plate. On the right, shiny, engraved silver caps covered the small silver rice bowls, keeping the rice warm. Chopsticks and napkins completed the place settings.

In the middle of the table lay a platter full of *sashimi,* or raw fish. A rare treat, sashimi was one of Lisa's father's favorites. Using long serving chopsticks, each family member took several pieces for his or her plate, then dipped the fish in a tangy horseradish mustard (called *wasabi)* mixed with soy sauce, eating it with his or her fingers. The elder Kumakis ate pieces of pink ginger to clear their mouths of the last taste of fish. They took bites of rice with their chopsticks, always leaving the bowl on the table. Lisa was about to pour soy sauce on the rice and lift the bowl close to her mouth, but then she remembered: You pick up the soup, not the rice. She lifted the soup bowl with two hands and sipped the lukewarm soup, chewing on small pieces of tofu (soybean curd) and seaweed. Next to her, Lisa's father poured *sake,* or Japanese rice wine, into a small ceramic cup for her grandfather.

Japanese food has become popular in the United States because it is beautiful, healthful, and well prepared. Compared to Korean, Indian, or Thai food, Japanese food is delicately flavored, relying more on presentation than on strong flavors. *Sushi,* for example, is carefully designed by master chefs so that it is pleasing to the eye as well as to the tongue. The word *sushi* describes different forms of a rice and, usually, fish dish.

One popular dish is *maki.* Maki is made by touching strips of vegetable, egg, or fish with the wasabi, surrounding the strips with

WHAT NOT TO DO AT A JAPANESE MEAL

Symbolic Rules

• Do not leave chopsticks sticking up from a rice bowl. This symbolically honors the dead.

• Do not start eating until your seniors have picked up their chopsticks. The aged have higher status, so the younger must follow them.

Simple Good Manners

• Do not pick up with a chopstick large chunks of food that must be bitten off. Pull the food apart first and then take smaller bites, unless it is sushi, which may be eaten with the fingers.

• Do not hold the rice bowl up to your mouth and shove in rice with the chopsticks.

• Do not blow your nose, smack your lips, speak with your mouth full, or use toothpicks in public.

Eating Rice and Using Chopsticks

• Do not leave rice uneaten in your bowl.

• Do not use your own chopsticks to take food from the serving platters. Either use the serving chopsticks on the platters, or turn your own chopsticks around to use the other end.

• Do not hold your chopsticks while receiving a second serving. Put the chopsticks down and stop eating while you wait.

— Adapted from *Japanese Etiquette: An Introduction,* by the World Fellowship Committee of the Tokyo Young Women's Christian Association. Tokyo: Charles E. Tuttle Co., 1992.

This classic Japanese-style meal revolves around *sukiyaki* (center), a dish including beef sirloin, cubed tofu, and black mushrooms. Other dishes, shown clockwise from the upper right, include *otakuwan* (sliced pickled radish), rice, *horenso goma ae* (spinach with sesame-seed dressing), and *osenbei* (rice crackers).

rice, and wrapping them with seaweed. Popular forms of maki are *kappa maki,* made of cucumber, *tekka maki,* made of raw tuna, and the ever-popular California maki, made of avocado, crab, and delicate orange fish eggs. Maki is eaten in a single bite, after being dipped in a mixture of wasabi and soy sauce.

Sushi is eaten the same way, and although it is often classified along with maki, it is made differently. Sushi is made up of an oval-shaped ball of rice, spiced slightly with vinegar and smeared with wasabi paste, then topped with a slice of fresh, raw fish. Sushi may be eaten with chopsticks or fingers, dipped in a sauce, and finished in one bite. Fans of sushi preparation may sit at the sushi bar in a Japanese-style restaurant, watching the chef prepare each piece and ordering their dinners a piece at a time. Popular forms of sushi include *ebi,* or sweet shrimp; *anago,* or eel; and *hamachi,* or yellowtail. Sometimes, people eat a piece of *tamago,* or sweet-egg sushi, for dessert.

Tempura, another popular Japanese food, consists of deep-fried vegetables and shrimp. Long pieces of shrimp, whole beans, and sweet potato slices lean against one another in the shape of a teepee, surrounded on the platter by other golden-colored, crispy disks of fried onion, mushrooms, and eggplant. Tempura pieces are eaten with chopsticks, after being dipped in a bowl of soy sauce flavored with radish and ginger.

Not as well known among mainstream Americans but popular with many Asians is the noodle soup dish called *udon.* The fat, chewy, flat white noodles are made of wheat and usually served piping hot in soup. Because the noodles are so thick, udon must be eaten quickly, before they absorb the soup broth and become a soggy, squishy mess. Eating the noodles quickly with chopsticks means that you may make a slurping sound as you eat, which is perfectly acceptable during a Japanese meal. Udon noodles are often served with tempura, beef, or fish in the broth, along with grated vegetables on top.

Traditional Japanese Customs in an American Setting

The next day, after Josephine had left and Lisa's mother and father both went to work, Lisa's grandmother decided to teach Lisa two distinctive Japanese art forms. So Lisa spent the day learning about flower arranging and the traditional tea ceremony.

Flower Arranging. Flower arranging comes from the custom of offering flowers to Buddha and the Shinto gods. Just as importantly, though, this traditional art demonstrates the Japanese love of nature. In Western culture, blending colors beautifully is important in arranging flowers. In Japanese culture, beauty is found in the arrangement of the lines. For example, the branch, the stalk, and the shape of the flowers themselves are the first things Lisa's grandmother considers when she plans her flower arrangement. The three styles of flower arrangement are formal, natural, and modern.

In the formal style, the branches are shaped into the form of a triangle. The three sides of the triangle symbolize heaven, earth, and humans. The goal of this style is to show oneness and balance.

In the natural style, the flowers create a natural scene to blend with the shape of the container. Sometimes containers are low and

BENTO

One typical Japanese-style meal that is common in the United States is *bento,* a portable meal packed in a box. Although bento seems perfect for today's busy lifestyles, it originated during the sixteenth century in Japan with a feudal lord who wanted to serve a limited, simple meal to his servants. Old-style bentos were made up of a riceball, a pickle, and a tart plum wrapped in a leaf. Today, bentos are commonly filled with some combination of sushi, noodles served without broth, rice balls, dried fish, plums, chicken *teriyaki,* seasoned squares of tofu, or egg. Bento meals are served in many Japanese restaurants in American cities.

This combination of flowers, pine, and bamboo artfully celebrates the New Year. Flower arranging, a treasured Japanese art form, has survived the transition to the United States.

flat, for example, and the flowers may be grouped off to one side, as if they were a growth of plants on the edge of a river. The natural style is free and has no set form.

Finally, in the modern style, flowers flow from a tall vase. The goal of the modern form is for the arrangement to look as if the flowers were placed there freely. The flowers are always arranged carefully, however, in order to follow certain rules and to show harmony. Arrangements that look effortless are sometimes the most difficult of all to make.

Special flowers are used for different occasions. For example, for New Year's and weddings, flower arrangements use bamboo, pine, and flowering plum branches. Pine and rose symbolize joy; tree peony and bamboo symbolize wealth and peace; pine symbolizes eternal youth. Vases should be silver or bronze, or glazed in cool colors such as green and white. For the Doll Festival, an annual March celebration for girls, flowering peach and chrysanthemums are used. For the Children's Festival in May, iris is used to symbolize bravery and strength. Flowers are chosen to reflect the season in which they are used, their symbolism, and the length of time they remain fresh. Praising a flower arrangement is a gesture of respect. For sad occasions, such as funerals, no flower arrangement is used because there is nothing to celebrate.

The Tea Ceremony. The tea ceremony is a central part of Japanese culture, but it is not commonly practiced in private homes among Japanese Americans. However, because it symbolizes Japan so beautifully, Japanese American cultural centers, Buddhist temples, and Japanese schools teach the ceremony in formal lessons.

The tea ceremony symbolizes beauty, purity, and harmony. Every action, every color, every sound is chosen carefully to create a simple and natural experience. In fact, traditionally, the ceremony was held in special tea houses, something like straw huts, in the yards of traditional Japanese homes. A tea house is large enough to host five people; it has a special room to wash teacups and a waiting room from which guests are invited in.

Several occasions, based on time of day or natural events, are set for serving tea. Some traditional teas are scheduled according to the day's schedule, such as morning, noontime, after dinner, or evening times. Special teas may be held to appreciate natural beauty, such as the Moon, Snow, Autumn, or Flower Ceremonies. Still others commemorate the New Year, memorials, or farewells to special friends.

Traditionally, a man conducts the tea ceremony, although this practice is not commonly followed in the Japanese American community. Several steps make up the ceremony. First, the host sends the invitations. Guests gather and await the host. When guests enter the tea room, they bow and seat themselves according to social status. The host first shares a small meal, serving sake (rice wine) and rice to the guests. After offering soup and special small cakes to the guests, the host clears the dishes from the tea room. During this time, the guests may step outside to smoke. Then the host sounds a gong summoning the guests to tea.

First, thick tea is served from a bowl. Japanese teas are all made from green powdered tea leaves. The thick tea that is first served contains more powder and has a consistency that is much like that of pea soup. After the thick tea comes thin tea, which is made with less powder. This tea is often served with cakes. Following the tea ceremony, the guests must visit or write to their host within three or four days to thank him for the ceremony. The goals of a tea ceremony are to honor the guests, experience beauty and calmness, and behave in a reserved and modest manner. Small expressions of thoughtfulness, like

In this traditional-style room, a family shares tea. Each family member has removed his or her shoes and sits with legs folded under the body. Elderly grandparents appreciate these customs.

awaiting one's turn, complimenting the room, and thanking the host, are the most important acts a guest can perform.

Although traditional Japanese customs such as these are often taught or performed on special occasions, they are not part of the daily life of most young Japanese Americans. The young adult generation, the Sansei, and their children, the Yonsei (the fourth generation) are nearly as far removed from their ancestors' roots as are European Americans of, for example, German or Irish descent. But the Nisei, the second generation whose parents were born in Japan, often grew up in Japantowns. Because of these two factors, some Nisei are very aware of their Japanese heritage. They carefully teach it to their children. Others, out of sadness and fear resulting from the internment during World War II, have pushed aside their Japanese roots in a quest to fit in better with mainstream American life.

In either case, because of the many years Japanese Americans have lived in the United States, most third- and fourth-generation Japanese Americans live a life just like that of most mainstream Americans. In addition, marriage to non-Japanese Americans has contributed to a mainstream lifestyle for many Sansei and their children.

Some exceptions to this pattern include Japanese Americans in Hawaii, where the history is different; some Japanese Americans on the West Coast, where their numbers are larger and their history inescapable; and other Japanese Americans who particularly value their background. By attending or sending their children to Japanese cultural events at Buddhist temples, Japanese schools, and groups like the Japanese American Service Committees, these Americans keep the ties to their heritage strong — in the face of a history that has strained against those ties.

Japanese American figure skater Kristi Yamaguchi displays her 1992 Olympic gold medal in Albertville, France. Her proud display and big smile show her American expressiveness and exuberance.

CHAPTER SIX

CONTRIBUTIONS TO AMERICAN CULTURE
FROM KARATE TO HAIKU TO CONGRESS

"**W**hy should we study Japanese?"

This was the question being debated in a junior high classroom. "So many people these days speak Spanish," argued one girl. "Even Roy, who says he's Japanese, doesn't speak any."

"My mom says we should study French. Or Latin."

"Well, the Japanese build great cars. What else do they do?"

The teacher spoke up. "Do you remember studying haiku in Language Arts? That's Japanese. Have you studied karate? That's Japanese. Have you ever eaten sushi? That's Japanese."

"But what does that have to do with America?"

"Many art forms from Japan have become part of our culture. So have many contributions made by Japanese Americans."

"But Japanese Americans are Americans, right?"

"Right, they are Americans, but as a group they have contributed scientific discoveries, important writing, and leadership. There is more to Japanese heritage in the United States than meets the eye."

A Variety of Contributions

When the first-generation Issei sailed to the U.S. mainland to work and make their fortunes, they brought with them distinctive cultural traditions. Buddhism, Japanese food, and service to the elderly have enriched American religious, cultural, and social life. But other common activities are also Japanese in origin, such as the art of folding paper called origami; haiku poetry; the unique form of theater known as Kabuki; and the well-known discipline of karate.

In Japan, and often in Japanese American culture, a strong tradition of love for nature and beauty has persisted for centuries. Underneath a seemingly simple art form is a highly developed art that sends a powerful message to the viewer. The simple forms of origami and haiku poetry make them popular among even mainstream American children. Other art forms, such as kabuki theater, are less simple and are more popular among adults.

Origami. Origami is an ancient Japanese art of folding paper into beautiful forms. Forms made of paper have long been used in Japan to celebrate special occasions, such as the doll festival. But origami is not limited to traditional Japanese customs. With thin, beautifully colored sheets of paper, Japanese American as well as other American children fold paper carefully into shapes resembling birds, lobsters, dolls, fans, boxes, flowers, hats, and fortune tellers. One especially important shape is the crane, which symbolizes peace, long life, and good health. Especially popular with children in elementary and middle schools, simple origami is easy to learn, inexpensive, and great fun.

Haiku Poetry. Haiku, a form of poetry developed in urban Japan centuries ago as entertainment, has become a standard subject in language arts classes. In the original Japanese, its simple form is made up of seventeen syllables divided among three lines (five syllables in the first line, seven syllables in the middle line, and five syllables in the last line). Each haiku must also include a reference to nature and one particular event occurring in the present. These rules help teachers give students limits and standards for writing that even young people can understand and fulfill.

Kabuki Theater. Kabuki originated in Japan after the 1600s, when the nation's power shifted to Japan's great cities. Born as a form of temple entertainment, Kabuki performances are extreme, stylish, and challenging. Traditionally in Japan, men take women's roles, but in the United States, women also perform Kabuki with intensity and confidence.

Popularized in parts of the United States by master Shozo Sato of the University of Illinois, Kabuki's style is very formal, similar in a way to European opera. For example, when the star arrives on stage, he or she will stop part of the distance across the stage and strike a dramatic pose long before speaking. Fight scenes are staged with brave feats of dance-like violence. Makeup is done in brilliant colors, often red and white. The performers' voices range up and down the scale in a manner that sounds at times like yelling, at other times like singing, and at other times like painful mourning. Actors pause in exaggerated poses to deliver their lines for a powerful effect.

In a blending of Japanese and European-style art forms, Kabuki versions of Western dramas have been performed throughout the United States. Some Kabuki-style performances include *Hansel and Gretel,* after the German folk tale in which an evil stepmother tries to kill her stepchildren; *Medea,* after the ancient Greek drama of a woman who loses her husband and murders her children; and *Othello,* a version of the Shakespearean drama about the Moorish warrior who is deceived into killing his beloved wife.

The Physical and Mental Discipline of Karate. Training in the Japanese martial art of karate has helped many non-Japanese American women, children, and men gain confidence, strength, and power in character as well as body. *Dojos,* or studios teaching karate, are common in every U.S. city.

HAIKU: POETRY FOR PEOPLE OF ALL CULTURES

Haiku is a classical form of poetry that brings beauty in a natural way to people of many cultures and ages.

Here is an example of Japanese haiku, by Matsuo Basho, called "Lightning at Night": "A lightning gleam: / into darkness travels / a night heron's scream."

Members of the Issei generation wrote haiku to express some of the difficulties of life in America. One woman wrote to describe her awful weariness after working in the fields all day and doing housekeeping all night: "Vexed beyond my strength, I wept. And then the wind came, drying up all tears."

Excellent examples of haiku have also been written by American schoolchildren, including this poem by Gay Weiner when she was in the fourth grade: "Gold, brown, and red leaves all twirling and scattering as the children play."

Students limber up before a judo class. Judo, like other Japanese martial arts, relies on concentration more than on physical strength.

Karate was created to overcome weaknesses. Unlike fighting, karate helps a person to act out of deeply held beliefs or love for others or country. This love brings the strength of decisiveness, allowing a person to overcome barriers, such as fear. With proper focus, even small or weak people can become powerful. Karate's movements and techniques rely on this inner strength; its goal is perfect character, not perfect fighting.

Willing to Be the First

Perhaps because of their long and challenging experiences in the United States, Japanese Americans have pioneered in many fields. After the Chinese, Japanese Americans were the first Asian immigrants to come to this country. Unlike many other Asian immigrants, primarily those from Southeast Asia who have arrived in great numbers since the 1960s, Japanese Americans have participated in American life for a century.

Many Japanese Americans are descended from established, well-educated farming families. They hold high standards for themselves and for their communities. This legacy lives on in the achievements of their descendants, including groundbreaking work in agriculture, the sciences, and communications. As a result of their unjust imprisonment during World War II, a legacy of political leadership on civil rights issues has become part of the Japanese American heritage as well. Japanese Americans have also contributed to mainstream culture by participating in the arts and by making great discoveries in science.

A farmer and his granddaughter plant onions, continuing a tradition that spans generations of Japanese Americans. Resourceful Japanese American farmers grew crops where many other Americans could not.

West Coast Agricultural Inventiveness

Backed by a centuries-long history of working with limited land and short seasons in Japan, Japanese American farmers contributed to the West Coast farming economy in many ways. They converted barren land into productive and profitable farms, including orchards and vineyards. To do this, they experimented with using new irrigation techniques, intensive labor, and their own ingenuity. For example, Japanese American farmers raised the first commercial crop of rice in California. Many of California's fruit and vegetable farmers were also Japanese.

In 1910, they produced two-thirds of California's strawberries, and by 1940, they were growing nearly half of California's onions and green peas, two-thirds of its fresh tomatoes, and 95 percent of its fresh snap peas. They supplied local markets in Los Angeles, Fresno, and San Francisco.

In 1909, 120 of 180 produce stalls in the Los Angeles City Market were owned by Japanese. In 1920, the agricultural production of Japanese farms was valued at 10 percent of the total value of California's crops. Seeking to broaden their horizons and prove what they could contribute, Japanese Americans planted acres of grapes, fruit trees, alfalfa, and hay in desolate Yosemite. In their earthy, diligent manner, early Japanese Americans thus contributed to the economy and well being of California and other parts of the West.

Discoveries

Japanese Americans have long excelled in the sciences. During the 1970s, two Issei won Nobel Prizes for their contributions. Leo Esaki of New York won the Nobel Prize in physics for his electron tunneling theories, and Tetsuo Akutso pioneered the development of artificial hearts. In addition, Harvey Itano won the Reverend Dr. Martin Luther King Medical Achievement Award for his outstanding contributions to the research on sickle cell anemia, a disease that primarily affects African Americans.

The work of Japanese Americans has improved the quality, and sometimes the length, of life for many other Americans as well. Recently, Douglas Ishii of Colorado State University identified a possible cause of the complications from diabetes that often cause blindness and loss of limbs.

Japanese Americans, such as Ellison Onizuka, have been pioneers in other areas of science as well. The first Asian American astronaut, Onizuka was a crew member on the ill-fated space shuttle *Challenger* that exploded during flight in 1986. He was tragically killed along with the rest of the crew.

Popular Entertainers

Japanese Americans have carved out niches in all areas of the media, from silent movies to television reporting. They have written

New York physicist Dr. Leo Esaki smiles with his wife after winning the 1973 Nobel Prize for physics.

books of fiction and nonfiction, published stories for children, and written plays. Sessue Hayakawa was a film star of the 1920s and 1930s silent movie era. George Takei played a major role as Sulu in the first "Star Trek" television series; he has appeared in many movies, is active in Los Angeles politics, and recently published his autobiography. Pat Morita has

George Takei starred as Sulu in the television show "Star Trek." He is now an activist in the Asian American community.

starred in the *Karate Kid* movies, had a regular role as Arnold in the 1970s television series "Happy Days," and performs as a stand-up comic. Robert Sato assisted Jack Klugman in the series "Quincy" and performed in the movie *Star Trek: The Next Generation.* The father of Margaret Cho's character in the television series "All-American Girl" is played by Clyde Kusatu, who has also acted in many television and movie roles, including episodes of "M*A*S*H."

There is a long list of movie actors who are of Japanese American descent. Tamlin Tomita starred in *The Joy Luck Club.* Miyoshi Umeki, in addition to acting in the series "The Courtship of Eddie's Father," performed in Rogers and Hammerstein's *Flower Drum Song* and was nominated for an Oscar. Makoto "Mako" Iwamatsu acted in the movie *Rising Sun,* among many other performances. One face that is familiar to millions of television viewers is that of Jack Soo, who was a part of the long-running "Barney Miller" television series. After World War II, when anti-Japanese sentiment was common, Soo feared being discriminated against, so he changed his name from Suzuki to the Chinese-sounding Soo.

Japanese American television journalists are also being seen in major mar-

Actor Pat Morita wears a traditional Japanese robe over a 1970s-style American shirt. For decades, Morita has starred in such hit movies and television shows as *The Karate Kid* and "Happy Days."

Actors Jack Soo and Romi Yamada Li promote the nightclub version of the hit Broadway and movie musical, *The Flower Drum Song.* Soo is best known for his role in the long-running television hit "Barney Miller."

kets from Hawaii to Colorado to Chicago to New York. They include Adele Arakawa from Chicago and Kent Ninomiya, originally from California.

Writing New Stories

Japanese American writers are breaking new ground in telling stories to mainstream Americans. Historians, adult literary writers, and children's book writers and publishers are paving a road for other, newer ethnic groups to follow. First of all, Japanese Americans have written innovative and exceptional histories. Ronald Takaki, a historian at the University of California at

Myoshi Umeki won an Oscar for her role in the film *Sayonara.* Later, she starred in the popular television series "The Courtship of Eddie's Father."

Hiroshima is a successful American jazz band that uses Japanese musical elements. For example, June Kuramoto plays the *koto*, a traditional stringed instrument that she studied for years. Johnny Mori plays the *taiko*, Japanese festival drums, and teaches others to play them. Neither instrument has ever been used before in American jazz. Hiroshima was nominated for a Soul Train Music Award, their music has been played in the Jazz Top 10, and they have received an Emmy and a Grammy, among other awards. Their albums include *Hiroshima, Odori, Another Place,* and *Go.* African Americans, mainstream Americans, and Asian Americans all attend their concerts and buy their recordings. By adding music from their heritage, they have enriched American jazz.

Sandra Yamate, a publisher of multicultural literature for children, conducts business by phone at her home. Like Yamate, many Japanese Americans have pioneered for change in our culture.

Berkeley, was nominated for a Pulitzer Prize. His work includes a book on multicultural America titled *A Different Mirror* and the critically acclaimed *Iron Cages: Race and Culture in Nineteenth-Century America.* Bill Hosokawa, a Nisei historian, has written about his generation as well as a history of all Japanese Americans titled *East to America.* Many other Japanese Americans have written about their history, especially the World War II internment.

In addition to writing about the past, Japanese Americans write for the future. Some Japanese Americans focus on books for children. In the 1950s, Jun Atsushi Iwamatsu (the father of actor Mako Iwamatsu) wrote children's books, including *Crow Boy, Umbrella,* and *Seashore Story,* all of which were runners-up for the prestigious Caldecott award. Sandra Yamate, a Chicago attorney-turned-publisher, has founded a multicultural children's book publishing company that tells stories for American children about life outside the mainstream. Books she has written include *Ashok by Any Other Name* and *Char Siu Bao Boy.* She has also published books about Filipino Americans, Korean Americans, and the Japanese internment.

As with other U.S. ethnic groups, such as Irish Americans, African Americans, and Jewish Americans, Japanese American adult literary writers focus on their group's experience. Lydia Minatoya wrote *Talking to High Monks in the Snow: An Asian American Odyssey,* a memoir about her struggles to straddle two cultures. Minatoya is a winner of the 1991 PEN/Jerard Fund Award, and her work has won praise from critics across the country. Sansei poet David Mura, in *Turning Japanese,* wrote about finding his Japanese identity despite living as an American for his entire life.

A distinctive Japanese American author is Phillip Kan Gotanda, who wrote the poignant and funny play, *Yankee Dog You Die,* dealing with the pain of being an outsider in American culture. Kyoko Mori, a teacher of creative writing in Wisconsin, has written short stories, poems, and a warmly reviewed memoir, *The Dream of Water,* about returning to Japan after a lifetime spent in the United States. Her first novel — a book for young readers called *Shizuko's Daughter* — was also highly praised by critics. Karen Tei Yamashita, from Cali-

Author Kyoko Mori signs copies of her memoir, *The Dream of Water,* at a bookstore. Many Japanese American writers reflect on the experience of seeking homes in two cultures.

fornia, writes about Japanese who live in South America. Other novels by Japanese American writers include *All I'm Asking for Is My Body,* by Milton Murayama; *Songs My Mother Taught Me,* by Wakako Yamauchi; *Go,* by Holly Uyemoto; and *A Bridge Between Us,* by Julie Shigekuni, which deals with relationships between mothers and daughters across four generations. Japanese American literature is

Former San Jose Mayor Norman Mineta plays baseball with his young son. As a child, Mineta was interned during World War II; he now participates in national politics.

as diverse as the individuals who create it and as fresh as their vision of the United States.

Political Leaders

Many Japanese American political leaders share their Japanese heritage, residence in Hawaii or California, and an awareness of the needs of Asian Americans, other minorities, and the nation's well being in general. These leaders have been motivated by their long residence in the United States, their suffering under discrimination, and their high levels of achievement. They and other Japanese Americans are helping to open the doors to political activism for the wave of Asian Americans who have moved to the United States in the last thirty years.

Senator Daniel Inouye, a senior Democrat, serves from Hawaii. As former Chair of the Senate Subcommittee on Communica-

tions, he has been a leader in forming laws for our new era of computer communication. In addition, as Chair of the Indian Affairs Committee, he dealt with controversial issues concerning Indian gaming. He also sponsored the National Disaster Protection Act to help the nation plan ways to better cope with natural disasters.

Bob Matsui, a congressional representative from California, helped pass an important trade law (NAFTA, the North American Free Trade Agreement) when President Bill Clinton's administration was struggling to get it through Congress. Matsui also pushed to get more Asian Americans appointed to high office in the Clinton Administration. They included Dennis Hayashi as head of civil rights activities for the Department of Health and Human Services and Paul Igesaki as Equal Employment Opportunity Commissioner. Their presence in Washington has helped illustrate the United States' growing diversity.

Congressional representative Norman Mineta of California helped create the Asian Pacific Islander Caucus, the first-ever Congressional leadership group on Asian American issues. He argued in front of the Japanese American Citizens League in favor of same-sex marriages, which the JACL then endorsed. Among political leaders, advocates for gay and lesbian rights are rare indeed.

Phil Tajitsu Nash is the executive director of the National Asian Pacific American Legal Consortium (NAPACL). The NAPACL is the country's first national umbrella advocacy group for Asian Americans. Nash is a spokesperson for issues ranging from immigration to civil rights to anti-Asian violence.

Many of these leaders act from the belief that when minorities protest against acts of discrimination, all Americans benefit from increased freedom in their daily lives. All of these leaders, and hundreds of others who are active on the local level, show mainstream America that its culture has more than one complexion, one background, or one way of solving problems.

Japanese American language, culture, writing, discoveries, leadership, and industriousness affect American life everyday. In the nation's midst is a brilliant, dynamic culture that uniquely blends East and West, offering Americans a new vision of themselves. Japanese Americans, among other cultures of America, will help to provide a direction for the next century.

A crowd of Americans from a variety of ethnic and cultural backgrounds attend a Japanese-style festival. Japanese culture has been bringing richness and diversity to the United States for more than a century.

CHRONOLOGY

1603-1858	The Edo Period takes place in Japan, during which Japan strengthens its native culture.
1639	Japan begins a period of isolation from the West.
1868	The Meiji Restoration takes place; new reforms occur that open Japan to the West, changing Japanese culture and opening the door to emigration; the Meiji Period lasts until 1911; most Japanese emigration takes place during this period of openness.
1868	The Hawaiian consul general in Japan begins secretly recruiting Japanese laborers.
1872	The Meiji government decides that "girls should be educated . . . alongside boys."
1880s	Japan's first generation of immigrants begins arriving in Hawaii.
1884	Japanese government allows the Hawaiian consul general to openly recruit laborers.
1885-1924	200,000 Japanese emigrate to Hawaii; 180,000 emigrate to the U.S. mainland.
1900	Hawaii becomes a territory of the United States.
1904-1905	The Russo-Japanese War takes place, encouraging young Japanese men to leave Japan to avoid fighting against Russia.
1906-1905	The School Crisis takes place in San Francisco as a result of the earthquake, leading to a ban on migration of Japanese to the U.S. mainland.
1907-1908	The "Gentleman's Agreement" is reached, prohibiting Japanese in Hawaii from moving to the U.S. mainland.
1909	The California legislature considers seventeen anti-Japanese measures; the Alien Land Law, which prohibits all non-citizens from owning land in California, is signed into law; this law prevents Japanese immigrant farmers from owning the land that they farmed; because they are not white, they are not eligible to ever become citizens.
1913	The California legislature considers over thirty anti-Japanese bills.
1921	The "Ladies' Agreement" prohibits immigration of picture brides from Japan to the United States.
1924	The Japanese Exclusion Act is made law, prohibiting any immigration by Japanese to the United States; with the passage of this Act, immigration of picture brides comes to a halt.
1930	A group of Nisei professionals form the Japanese American Citizens League.
1941	December 7: Japan's navy bombs Pearl Harbor, Hawaii; in direct response, the United States enters World War II by declaring war on Japan.
1942	Acting out of its fear over the supposedly questionable loyalty of Japanese American citizens, the U. S. government transfers all Japanese Americans on the West Coast, including U.S.-born citizens who have never even been to Japan, to internment camps for the duration of World War II.
1945	World War II ends; Japanese Americans are released from the internment camps; the Japanese American population spreads throughout the United States.
1964	The Civil Rights Act becomes law, guaranteeing equal opportunities for Americans of every race, religion, or national origin.
1965	The Immigration Act opens up immigration to people of nonwhite origin.
1970s	Prominent Japanese American scientists win awards for science, including the Nobel Prize.

1988	The U.S. government formally apologizes and promises a payment to the survivors of the internment camps.
1992	Kristi Yamaguchi, a Japanese American skater, wins the Olympic Gold Medal for figure skating.
1995	Hideo Nomo, a star pitcher in his native Japan, celebrates his rookie year in the major leagues by starting for the National League All-Star team; the first Japanese player to make a U.S. All-Star team, Nomo throws two scoreless innings and strikes out four; known as "The Tornado" because of his unorthodox "twister" delivery, Nomo excites baseball fans across North America; he is also a source of pride for Japanese Americans, who turn out in droves to watch him play for the Los Angeles Dodgers.

GLOSSARY

Buddhism	An important religion in Japan dating from the sixth century.
Edo Period	A period lasting from 1600 to 1867, during which Japan was closed to outside influence and developed a distinctive national culture.
Emigrants	People who leave one country to go and live in another.
Ginger	A peppery spice used to decorate and flavor sushi.
Haiku	A short, simple poem with limited syllables focusing on nature.
Immigrants	People who come to one country from another.
Internment	A synonym for imprisonment.
Isolationism	The tendency of a nation to refuse to interact with other nations.
Issei	The first generation of Japanese immigrants.
Kibei	Born in the United States, Japanese Americans who returned to Japan for their educations.
Labor unions	Groups of workers who support one another while pursuing better wages and working conditions.
Lunas	The overseers, or bosses, on Hawaiian sugar plantations.
Mainland, U.S.	The forty-eight contiguous U.S. states (that is, excluding Alaska and Hawaii) south of the U.S.-Canadian border.
Meiji Period	A period lasting from 1868 to 1911, during which most Japanese emigrated to Hawaii and the U.S. mainland.
Migration	The movement of a people.
Modernization	The efforts made by the Meiji government to move Japan into modern Western culture by opening trade, expanding education, and developing industry.
Nisei	The second generation of Japanese immigrants; children of Issei.
Origami	The art of folding paper into special shapes, such as herons or cranes.
Picture brides	Japanese women who came to the United States to marry men from Japan; the marriages were arranged with photographs of the women and men serving as the primary means of introduction.
Recruiters	Agents of the Hawaiian sugar plantations who went to Japan to encourage young people to migrate to the islands to work.

Redress	The U.S. government's admission of wrongdoing in interning Japanese Americans during World War II.
Russo-Japanese War	A war that took place between Russia and Japan during 1904-1905.
Sake	A strong rice wine served in delicate ceramic cups.
Samurai	The warrior class that ruled the peasants during the Edo Period.
Sansei	The third generation of Japanese immigrants; grandchildren of Issei.
Sashimi	A special dish of raw fish, served very fresh and carefully presented with hot mustard paste, soy sauce, and slices of ginger.
Settlers	Immigrants to the United States who decided to make this country their home.
Shinto	Japan's ancient, native religion.
Sojourners	Immigrants to the United States who planned to stay a period to work and then return to their native land.
Stereotypes	Simplified and limiting ideas about groups of people.
Sushi	A seaweed and rice roll with raw fish, vegetables, or other ingredients in the center.
Tempura	A batter-fried dish of vegetables or shrimp.
Typhoon	A tropical tornado occurring in Japan during summer and autumn.
Yonsei	The fourth generation of Japanese Americans.

FURTHER READING

A. Magazine: An Asian American Quarterly. New York: Metro East Publishers.

Chambers, Kevin. *Asian Customs and Manners.* New York: Meadowbrook, 1988.

Chuman, Frank F. *The Bamboo People: The Law and Japanese-Americans.* Chicago: Japanese American Research Project by the Japanese American Citizens League.

Japan as It Is. Tokyo: Gakken Co., 1990.

Minatoya, Lydia. *Talking to High Monks in the Snow: An Asian American Odyssey.* New York: HarperCollins Publishers, 1992.

Sarasohn, Eileen Sunada, ed. *The Issei: Portrait of a Pioneer. An Oral History.* Palo Alto, California: Pacific Books, 1983.

Statler, Oliver, intro. *All Japan: The Catalogue of Everything Japanese.* New York: Quill, 1984.

Sugiyama, S. *Basic Principles of Karate.* Chicago: Sugiyama Karate Dojo, 1991.

Takaki, Ronald. *Strangers from a Different Shore: A History of Asian Americans.* New York: Penguin Books, 1989.

Wilson, Robert A. and Bill Hosokawa. *East to America: A History of the Japanese in the United States.* New York: William Morrow and Company, 1980.

INDEX